Break Away

Robin Pearson

Debbie J. Chambers

OXFORD
UNIVERSITY PRESS

1904 ❧ 2004

100 YEARS OF
CANADIAN PUBLISHING

OXFORD
UNIVERSITY PRESS

8 Sampson Mews, Suite 204, Don Mills, Ontario M3C 0H5
www.oupcanada.com

Oxford University Press is a department of the University of Oxford.

It furthers the University's objective of excellence in research, scholarship, and education by publishing worldwide in

Oxford New York
Auckland Bangkok Buenos Aires Cape Town Chennai
Dar es Salaam Delhi Hong Kong Istanbul Karachi Kolkata
Kuala Lumpur Madrid Melbourne Mexico City Mumbai Nairobi
São Paulo Shanghai Taipei Tokyo Toronto

Oxford is a registered trade mark of Oxford University Press
in the UK and in certain other countries

Published in Canada
by Oxford University Press

National Library of Canada Cataloguing in Publication Data

Break Away: Reading and Writing for Success /
[compiled by] Robin Pearson and Debbie J. Chambers.

For use in grade 12.
ISBN 978-0-19-542095-1

1. Readers (Secondary). I. Pearson, Robin II. Chambers, Debbie J., 1969-

PE1121.B74 2004   428.6   C2004-900165-5

Printed and bound in the United States

11 12 – 17 16

Publisher: Janice Schoening
Managing editor: Monica Schwalbe
Developmental editor: Chelsea Donaldson
Copy editor: Karen Alliston
Production editor: Niki Walker
Photo research and permissions: Paula Joiner
Cover design: Brett Miller
Cover image: Kim Westerskov/Getty Images
Text design and formatting: PageWave Graphics Inc.

ACKNOWLEDGEMENTS

We would like to thank our families, for their patience with the demands of this project, and also our students, from whom we have learned so much.

—*Robin Pearson and Debbie J. Chambers*

The publisher would like to acknowledge the following teachers and their students for their assistance in the development of this text:

- Jim Chevalier, Cardinal Carter Catholic Secondary School, Leamington, Ontario
- Rachel Cooke, York Memorial Collegiate, Toronto, Ontario
- Shelley Cooke, St. Peter's Secondary School, Peterborough, Ontario
- Cecelia Coulas, Acton District High School, Acton, Ontario
- Liliana Meschino, St. Basil-The-Great College School, Toronto, Ontario
- Chad Mowbray, Englehart High School, Englehart, Ontario

Every possible effort has been made to trace the original source of the text material contained in this book. Where the attempt has been unsuccessful, the publisher would be pleased to hear from the copyright holders to rectify any omissions.

Contents

Unit One: Fresh Perspectives

A Whack on the Side of the Head......4
Roger Van Oech
Informational text

All I Really Need to Know I Learned
in Kindergarten 14
Robert Fulghum
Personal essay

The 7 Habits of Highly
Effective Teens.................18
Sean Covey
Informational text

The 12 Rules About Hiring
and Firing 26
Richard Bolles
Graphic text

Want to Do Better on the Job?
Listen Up! 29
Diane Cole
Magazine article

Fabiola da Silva's X-traordinary
Career 32
Susan Carpenter
Newspaper article

X Games IX Schedules 36
Web page/Graphic text

Sammy Sosa 41
Profile

Sammy Sosa: Batting Statistics.......46
Graphic text

Kids Are the Forgotten Consumers ...48
Zoe Anderson-Jenkins
Personal essay

The Tiniest Guitar in the World......51
Martha Brooks
Short story

The Search for the Perfect Body......60
Mary Walters Riskin
Magazine article

To Christine 65
Susan Forde
Poem

Eating Disorders Poster 67
Graphic text

Special K Ad 69
Graphic text

Murder Revealed 71
Pat Hancock
Narrative account

Barney.....................75
Will Stanton
Fictional diary

Reflecting on Your Learning........79

Unit Two: Belonging to Communities

Small Town Ways 82
  June Chua
  Personal essay

Small Town 85
  John Cougar Mellencamp
  Song lyric

Case Study: Kensington Market,
  Toronto 88
  Colin M. Bain
  Textbook excerpt

The United Way 91
  Graphic text

The Urban Indian 95
  Drew Hayden Taylor
  Personal essay

I Grew Up 98
  Lenore Keeshig-Tobias
  Poem

Suitcase Lady 101
  Christie McLaren
  Newspaper article

The "Scream" School of Parenting . . . 104
  William Bell
  Short story

Canadian Families Changing 114
  Guenther Zuern
  Informational text

Our Cultural Diversity 117
  Colin M. Bain
  Textbook excerpt

Reach Out and Touch 120
  Maxine Tynes
  Poem

Japanese Canadians: Wartime
  Persecution 122
  Textbook excerpt

Teen Loitering: What the Heck Are
  They Up To? 125
  Vijay Narasimhan
  Magazine article

To Drive or Not To Drive 128
  Advice column

Traffic Signs 132
  Graphic text

Rising Car Insurance Hits
  Young Men Hardest 135
  Peter Cheney and Paul Waldie
  Newspaper article

Insurance Rates 139
  Graphic Text

"I Promise" Drives Safety 141
  Mike Pettapiece
  Newspaper article

The Day They Invented
  the Skateboard 145
  Bob Schmidt
  Memoir

Frontside Forces and Fakie
  Flight: The Physics of
  Skateboarding Tricks 149
  Pearl Tesler and Paul Doherty
  Informational text

Internet Statistics 154
  Web page

A Virtual Prom 156
  Cynthia Cho
  Newspaper article

Starr 160
  Angela Johnson
  Short story

Reflecting on Your Learning 167

Unit Three: Making a Difference

Ending the Blame Game 170
   Roberta Beecroft
   Informational text

The Living Years 173
   Mike Rutherford and B.A. Robertson
   Song lyric

Johnnie's Poem 176
   Alden Nowlan
   Poem

Steps to a Better Life 178
   Graphic text

The Scoop 180
   Web page

Smoking: Not a Cheap Thrill 184
   Informational text

Costs of Smoking 186
   World Health Organization
   Graphic text

The Underground Railroad 189
   J. Bradley Cruxton and W. Douglas Wilson
   Textbook excerpt

Changing the World 194
   Sharon Sterling and Steve Powrie
   Textbook excerpt

It Starts with Me 198
   Craig Kielburger
   Narrative essay

A Call to Volunteer 202
   Graphic text

Four Who Make a Difference 204
   Jennifer Burke Crump
   Magazine article

Bright Idea 213
   Guenther Zuern
   Magazine article

The Real McCoy 216
   Bev Spencer
   Profile

Safer Hockey 218
   Bev Spencer
   Narrative essay

Teens Make Their Own Peace 220
   Leah Eskin
   Magazine article

Kim Phuc 223
   David M.R.D. Spencer
   Biography

Address at the Vietnam War
Memorial 226
   Kim Phuc
   Speech

Forgiveness 228
   Jennifer Boehm
   Poem

The Bully 230
   Gregory Clark
   Short story

I am Canadian 234
   Master Corporal Frank Misztal
   Informational text

G.I. Jane? 236
   Veronica T.
   Personal essay

Travel Counsellors 239
   Informational text

Ecotourism Entrepreneur 242
   Colin M. Bain
   Profile

SUV Ad 244
   Graphic text

Ford Ad 246
   Ad Graphic text

Reflecting on Your Learning 249

Text and Figure Credits 250

Photo Credits 252

Fresh Perspectives

So much depends on how you look at things! The readings in this unit will challenge you to view yourself and your world differently. You'll learn about the importance of looking beyond the one "right" answer, consider how some simple habits can change the way you see your life, find out about people who have defied expectations, and read stories in which things are not quite as they first appear. These selections will help you focus your goals and reach for the stars!

READING STRATEGY

*Before you read each section of this selection, look at the heading and any text that is set off in italics or boldface. Write a one-sentence **prediction** of what the section will be about. After you have read the section, go back to your prediction. Was it accurate?*

VOCABULARY PREVIEW

- probe
- stagnant
- subordinates
- conservative
- curious
- innovative

A Whack on the Side of the Head

❖ by Roger Van Oech

The Right Answer

Exercise: Five figures are shown below. Select the one that is different from the others.

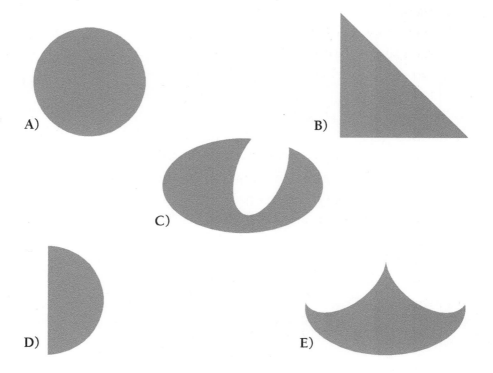

A)

B)

C)

D)

E)

Learning How to Think

Children enter school as question marks and leave as periods.
  —Neil Postman, Educator

Life can be like a big noisy party with people talking, music playing, and glasses clinking. But even with all this noise, it's possible for you to understand the person across from you. Or the one thirty feet [9 m] away. That's because our attention is selective—we can tune in certain things and tune out others.

See for yourself. Take a look around where you're sitting and find four things that have "red" in them. Go ahead and do it. With a "red" mindset, you'll find that red jumps right out at you: a red telephone book, red in the blister on your index finger, red in the wallpaper, and so on. Similarly, whenever you learn a new word, you hear it eight times in the next three days. In like fashion, you've probably noticed that after you get a new car, you see that make everywhere. That's because people find what they are looking for. If you look for beauty, you'll find beauty. If you look for conspiracies, you'll find conspiracies. It's all a matter of setting your mental channel.

Where do you learn how to set your mental channel? One important source is your formal education. There you learn what is appropriate and what is not. You learn many of the questions you use to probe your surroundings. You learn where to search for information, which ideas to pay attention to, and how to think about these ideas. Your educational training gives you many of the concepts you use to order and understand the world.

Speaking of education, how did you do on the five-figure exercise on the previous page? If you chose figure B, congratulations! You've picked the right answer. Figure B is the only one that has all straight lines. Give yourself a pat on the back!

Some of you, however, may have chosen figure C, thinking that C is unique because it's the only one that is asymmetrical. And you are also right! C is the right answer. A case can also be made for figure A: it's the only one with no points. Therefore, A is the right answer. What about D? It is the only one that has both a straight line and a curved line. So, D is the right answer too. And E? Among other things, E is the only one that looks like a projection of a non-Euclidean triangle into Euclidean space. It is also the right answer. In other words, they are all right depending on your point of view.

But you won't find this exercise in school. Much of our educational system is geared toward teaching people to find "the right answer." By the time the average person finishes college, he or she will have taken over 2600 tests, quizzes, and exams—many similar to the one you just took. The "right answer" approach becomes deeply ingrained in our thinking. This may be fine for some mathematical problems where there is in fact only one right answer. The difficulty is that most of life isn't this way. Life is ambiguous; there are many right answers—all depending on what you are looking for. But if you think there is only one right answer, then you'll stop looking as soon as you find one.

When I was a sophomore in high school, my English teacher put a small chalk dot like the one below on the blackboard.

She asked the class what it was. A few seconds passed and then someone said, "A chalk dot on the blackboard." The rest of the class seemed relieved that the obvious had been stated, and no one else had anything more to say. "I'm surprised at you," the teacher told the class. "I did the same exercise yesterday with a group of kindergartners, and they thought of fifty different things it could be: an owl's eye, a cigar butt, the top of a telephone pole, a star, a pebble, a squashed bug, a rotten egg, and so on. They had their imaginations in high gear."

In the ten-year period between kindergarten and high school, not only had we learned how to find the right answer, we had also lost the ability to look for more than one right answer. We had learned how to be specific, but we had lost much of our imaginative power.

Consequences

"I'm not returning until you fix it," bandleader Count Basie told a nightclub owner whose piano was always out of tune. A month later Basie got a call that everything was fine. When he returned, the piano was still out of tune. "You said you fixed it!" an irate Basie exclaimed. "I did," came the reply. "I had it painted."

The practice of looking for the "one right answer" can have serious consequences in the way we think about and deal with problems. Most people don't like problems, and when they encounter them, they usually react by taking the first way out they can find—even if they solve the wrong problem as did the nightclub owner in the above story. I can't overstate the danger in this. If you have only one idea, you have only one course of action open to you, and this is quite risky in a world where flexibility is a requirement for survival.

An idea is like a musical note. In the same way that a musical note can only be understood in relation to other notes (either as a part of a melody or a chord), an idea is best understood in the context of other ideas. If you have only one idea, you don't have anything to compare it to. You don't know its strengths and weaknesses. I believe that the French philosopher Emilé Chartier hit the nail squarely on the head when he said:

Nothing is more dangerous than an idea when it's the only one you have.

For more effective thinking, we need different points of view. Otherwise, we'll get stuck looking at the same things and miss seeing things outside our focus.

The Second Right Answer

A leading business school did a study that showed that its graduates performed well at first, but in ten years, they were overtaken by a more streetwise, pragmatic group. The reason according to the professor who ran the study: "We taught them how to solve problems, not recognize opportunities. When opportunity knocked, they put out their 'Do Not Disturb' signs."

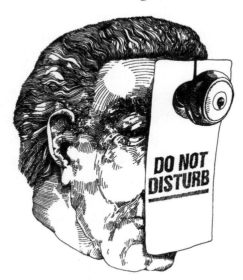

Not long ago I did a series of creative thinking workshops for the executive staff of a large computer company. The president had called me in because he was concerned about the stagnant thinking environment at the top. It seemed that whenever his subordinates would make a proposal, that's all they'd make—just one. They wouldn't offer any alternative ideas. Since they had been trained to look for the right answer, they usually didn't go beyond the first one they found. The president knew that it was easier to make good decisions if he had a variety of ideas from which to choose. He was also concerned with how conservative this "one-idea" tendency had made his people's thinking. If a person were presenting only one idea, he would generally propose the "sure thing" rather than take a chance on a less likely offbeat idea. This state of affairs created a less than ideal climate for generating innovative ideas. I told them that one way to be more creative is to:

Look for the second right answer.

Often, it is the second right answer which, although offbeat or unusual, is exactly what you need to solve a problem in an innovative way.

One technique for finding the second right answer is to change the questions you use to probe a problem. For example, how many times have you heard someone say, "What is the answer?" or "What is the meaning of this?" or "What is the result?" These people are looking for the answer, and the meaning, and the result. And that's all they'll find—just one. If you train yourself to ask questions that solicit plural answers like "What are the answers?" or "What are the meanings?" or "What are the results?" you will find that people will think a little more deeply and offer more than one idea. As the Nobel Prize winning chemist Linus Pauling put it:

**The best way to get a good
idea is to get a lot of ideas.**

You may not be able to use all of them, but out of the number you generate you may find a few that are worthwhile. This is why professional photographers take so many pictures when shooting an important subject. They may take twenty, sixty, or a hundred shots. They'll change the exposure, the lighting, the filters, and so on. That's because they know that out of all the pictures they take, there may be only a few that capture what they're looking for. It's the same thing with creative thinking: you need to generate a lot of ideas to get some good ones.

Inventor Ray Dolby (the man who took "hiss" out of recorded music) has a similar philosophy. He says:

> Inventing is a skill that some people have and some people don't. But you can learn how to invent. You have to have the will not to jump at the first solution, because the really elegant solution might be right around the corner. An inventor is someone who says, "Yes, that's one way to do it, but it doesn't seem to be an optimum solution." Then he keeps on thinking.

When you look for more than one right answer, you allow your imagination to open up. How do you keep a fish from smelling? Cook it as soon as you catch it. Freeze it. Wrap it in paper. Leave it in the water. Switch to chicken. Keep a cat around. Burn incense. Cut its nose off.

Change Your Question

The second assault on the same problem should come from a totally different direction.
—Tom Hirshfield, Physicist

Another technique for finding more answers is to change the wording in your questions. If an architect looks at an opening between two rooms and thinks, "What type of door should I use to connect these rooms?" that's what she'll design—a door. But if she thinks "What sort of passageway should I put here?" she may design something different like a "hallway," an "air curtain," a "tunnel," or perhaps a "courtyard." Different words bring in different assumptions and lead your thinking in different directions.

Here's an example of how such a strategy can work. Several centuries ago, a curious but deadly plague appeared in a small village in Lithuania. What was curious about this disease was its grip on its victim; as soon as a person contracted it, he'd go into a deep almost death-like coma. Most died within a day, but occasionally a hardy soul would make it back to the full bloom of health. The problem was that since eighteenth century medical technology wasn't very advanced, the unafflicted had quite a difficult time telling whether a victim was dead or alive.

Then one day it was discovered that someone had been buried alive. This alarmed the townspeople, so they called a town meeting to decide what should be done to prevent such a situation from happening again. After much discussion, most people agreed on the following solution. They decided to put food and water in every casket next to the body. They would even put an air hole from the casket up to the earth's surface. These procedures would be expensive, but they would be more than worthwhile if they would save people's lives.

Another group came up with a second, less expensive, right answer. They proposed implanting a twelve-inch long stake in every coffin lid directly over where the victim's heart would be. Then whatever doubts there were about whether the person was dead or alive would be eliminated as soon as the coffin lid was closed.

What differentiated the two solutions were the questions used to find them. Whereas the first group asked, "What should we do if we bury somebody alive?" the second group wondered, "How can we make sure everyone we bury is dead?"

I'd like to conclude this "right answer" chapter with one of my favourite Sufi stories.

Two men had an argument. To settle the matter, they went to a Sufi judge for arbitration. The plaintiff made his case. He was very eloquent and persuasive in his reasoning. When he finished, the judge nodded in approval and said, "That's right, that's right."

On hearing this, the defendant jumped up and said, "Wait a second, judge, you haven't even heard my side of the case yet." So the judge told the defendant to state his case. He, too, was very persuasive and eloquent. When he finished, the judge said, "That's right, that's right." When the clerk of court heard this, he jumped up and said, "Judge, they both can't be right." The judge looked at the clerk and said, "That's right, that's right."

Moral: Truth is all around you; what matters is where you place your focus.

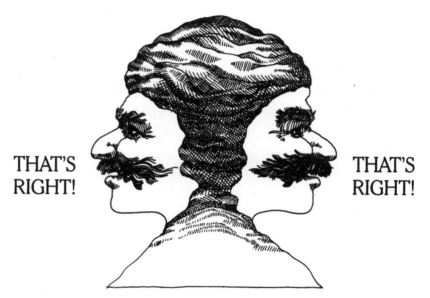

THAT'S RIGHT!   THAT'S RIGHT!

Summary

Much of our educational system has taught us to look for the one right answer. This approach is fine for some situations, but many of us have a tendency to stop looking for alternative right answers after the first right answer has been found. This is unfortunate because often it's the second, or third, or tenth right answer which is what we need to solve a problem in an innovative way.

There are many ways to find the second right answer—asking "what if," playing the fool, reversing the problem, breaking the rules, etc. The important thing, however, is to look for the second right answer, because unless you do, you won't find it.

Tip: The answers you get depend on the questions you ask. Play with your wording to get different answers. One technique is to solicit plural answers. Another is to ask questions that whack people's thinking. One woman told me that she had a manager who would keep her mind on its toes by asking questions such as: "What are three things you feel totally neutral about?" and "What parts of your problem do you associate with tax returns and what parts with poetry?"

ACTIVITIES

DIRECTLY STATED IDEAS AND INFORMATION

1. According to the author, what is the problem with thinking there is only one right answer to a problem?

2. Explain in your own words what the author means by "An idea is like a musical note" (page 7).

INDIRECTLY STATED IDEAS AND INFORMATION

3. What is the purpose of the exercise at the beginning of this selection?

4. Explain why you think "A Whack on the Side of the Head" is or is not a good title for this selection.

MAKING CONNECTIONS

5. In the last part of the selection, the author tells a story in which some townspeople come up with two ways to deal with the problem of burying people alive. Describe another strategy that they could have used to solve the problem.

WRITING EXTENSION

Write a one-page opinion piece to explain whether you think the educational system helps students become more creative or less creative. Use a T-chart to pre-plan your opinion piece. Give specific examples to back up your ideas.

READING STRATEGY

Before you read the selection below, jot down what you remember learning in kindergarten. As you read, see whether your experiences match those of the author.

VOCABULARY PREVIEW

- ◆ credo
- ◆ bland
- ◆ naïve
- ◆ brevity
- ◆ equality
- ◆ extrapolate

All I Really Need to Know I Learned in Kindergarten

❖ by Robert Fulghum

Each spring, for many years, I have set myself the task of writing a personal statement of belief: a Credo. When I was younger, the statement ran for many pages, trying to cover every base, with no loose ends. It sounded like a Supreme Court brief, as if words could resolve all conflicts about the meaning of existence.

The Credo has grown shorter in recent years—sometimes cynical, sometimes comical, sometimes bland—but I keep working at it. Recently I set out to get the statement of personal belief down to one page in simple terms, fully understanding the naïve idealism that implied.

The inspiration for brevity came to me at a gasoline station. I managed to fill an old car's tank with super-deluxe high-octane go-juice. My old hoopy couldn't handle it and got the willies— kept sputtering out at intersections and belching going downhill. I understood. My mind and my spirit get like that from time to time. Too much high-content information, and *I* get the existential willies—keep sputtering out at intersections where life choices must be made and I either know too much or not enough. The examined life is no picnic.

I realized then that I already know most of what's necessary to live a meaningful life—that it isn't all that complicated. *I know it.* And have known it for a long, long time. Living it—well, that's another matter, yes? Here's my Credo:

ALL I REALLY NEED TO KNOW about how to live and what to do and how to be I learned in kindergarten. Wisdom was not at the top of the graduate-school mountain, but there in a sandpile at Sunday School.

These are the things I learned:

- Share everything.
- Play fair.
- Don't hit people.
- Put things back where you found them.
- Clean up your own mess.
- Don't take things that are not yours.
- Say you're sorry when you hurt somebody.
- Wash your hands before you eat.
- Flush.
- Warm cookies and cold milk are good for you.
- Live a balanced life—learn some and think some and draw and paint and sing and dance and play and work every day some.
- Take a nap every afternoon.
- When you go out into the world, watch out for traffic, hold hands, and stick together.
- Be aware of wonder. Remember the little seed in the Styrofoam cup: The roots go down and the plant goes up and nobody really knows how or why, but we are all like that.
- Goldfish and hamsters and white mice and even the little seed in the Styrofoam cup—they all die. So do we.
- And remember the Dick-and-Jane books and the first word you learned—the biggest word of all—LOOK.

Everything you need to know is there somewhere. The Golden Rule and love and basic sanitation. Ecology and politics and equality and sane living.

Take any one of those items and extrapolate it into sophisticated adult terms and apply it to your family life or your work or your government or your world and it holds true and clear and firm. Think what a better world it would be if we all—the whole world—had cookies and milk about three o'clock every afternoon and then lay down with our blankies for a nap. Or if all governments had as a basic policy to always put things back where they found them and to clean up their own mess.

And it is still true, no matter how old you are—when you go into the world, it is best to hold hands and stick together.

ACTIVITIES

DIRECTLY STATED IDEAS AND INFORMATION

1. What does the author mean by the word "Credo"?

2. Where did the author find wisdom?

INDIRECTLY STATED IDEAS AND INFORMATION

3. Give two examples to illustrate what the author means when he says that governments should "put things back where they found them and . . . clean up their own mess."

4. Why does the author say it would be a better world if we all "had cookies and milk about three o'clock every afternoon and then lay down with our blankies for a nap"?

MAKING CONNECTIONS

5. Explain one thing you learned in kindergarten that the author didn't include in his list. How did this lesson help you be more successful as you grew older?

WRITING EXTENSION

Write a summary of this reading selection in 150 words or less. Make sure you use your own words. Include a clear main idea and at least two details that support the main idea.

Imagination is more important than knowledge.

— *Albert Einstein (1879–1955)*
Physicist and Philosopher

READING STRATEGY

Copy the **anticipation guide** below into your notebook. Before you read this selection, place a check mark in the first column next to any statement you agree with.

As you read, place check marks in the second column next to any statement that is backed up by the text. Record the page number and the paragraph where you found the information in the third column. What did you learn from the text that surprised you?

VOCABULARY PREVIEW

- ◆ effective
- ◆ victory
- ◆ renew
- ◆ proactive
- ◆ sequential

ANTICIPATION GUIDE	ME	TEXT	PROOF
1. Most of the time we are not aware of our habits.	___	___	___
2. Habits can be good, bad, or neutral.	___	___	___
3. Teens who are highly effective see life as a competition in which they will either be a winner or a loser.	___	___	___
4. Teens should start improving themselves in whatever "order" makes sense to them.	___	___	___

The 7 Habits of Highly Effective Teens

❖ by Sean Covey

Although I'm a retired teenager, I remember what it was like to be one. I could have sworn I was riding an emotional roller coaster most of the time. Looking back, I'm actually amazed that I survived. Barely. I'll never forget the time in seventh grade when I first fell in love with a girl named Nicole. I told my friend Clar to tell her that I liked her (I was too scared to speak directly to girls so I used interpreters). Clar completed his mission and returned and reported.

"Hey, Sean, I told Nicole that you liked her."

"What'd she say!?" I giggled.

"She said, 'Ooohhh, Sean. He's fat!'"

Clar laughed. I was devastated. I felt like crawling into a hole and never coming out again. I vowed to hate girls for life. Luckily my hormones prevailed and I began liking girls again.

I suspect that some of the struggles that teens have shared with me are also familiar to you:

"There's too much to do and not enough time. I've got school, homework, job, friends, parties, and family on top of everything else. I'm totally stressed out. Help!"

"How can I feel good about myself when I don't match up? Everywhere I look I am reminded that someone else is smarter, or prettier, or more popular. I can't help but think, 'If I only had her hair, her clothes, her personality, her boyfriend, then I'd be happy.'"

"I feel as if my life is out of control."

"My family is a disaster. If I could only get my parents off my back I might be able to live my life. It seems they're constantly nagging, and I can't ever seem to satisfy them."

"I know I'm not living the way I should. I'm into everything— drugs, drinking, sex, you name it. But when I'm with my friends, I give in and just do what everyone else is doing."

"I've started another diet. I think it's my fifth one this year. I really do want to change, but I just don't have the discipline to stick with it. Each time I start a new diet I have hope. But it's usually only a short time before I blow it. And then I feel awful."

"I'm not doing too well in school right now. If I don't get my grades up I'll never get into college."

"I'm moody and get depressed often and I don't know what to do about it."

These problems are real, and you can't turn off real life. So I won't try. Instead, I'll give you a set of tools to help you deal with real life. What are they? The 7 Habits of Highly Effective Teens or, said another way, the seven characteristics that happy and successful teens the world over have in common.

By now, you're probably wondering what these habits are so I might as well end the suspense. Here they are, followed by a brief explanation:

Habit 1:   Be Proactive
Take responsibility for your life.

Habit 2:   Begin with the End in Mind
Define your mission and goals in life.

Habit 3:   Put First Things First
Prioritize, and do the most important things first.

Habit 4:   Think Win-Win
Have an everyone-can-win attitude.

Habit 5:   Seek First to Understand, Then to Be Understood
Listen to people sincerely.

Habit 6:   Synergize
Work together to achieve more.

Habit 7:   Sharpen the Saw
Renew yourself regularly.

As the diagram on the next page shows, the habits build upon each other. Habits 1, 2, and 3 deal with self-mastery. We call it the "private victory." Habits 4, 5, and 6 deal with relationships and teamwork. We call it the "public victory." You've got to get your personal act together before you can be a good team player. That's why the private victory comes before the public victory.

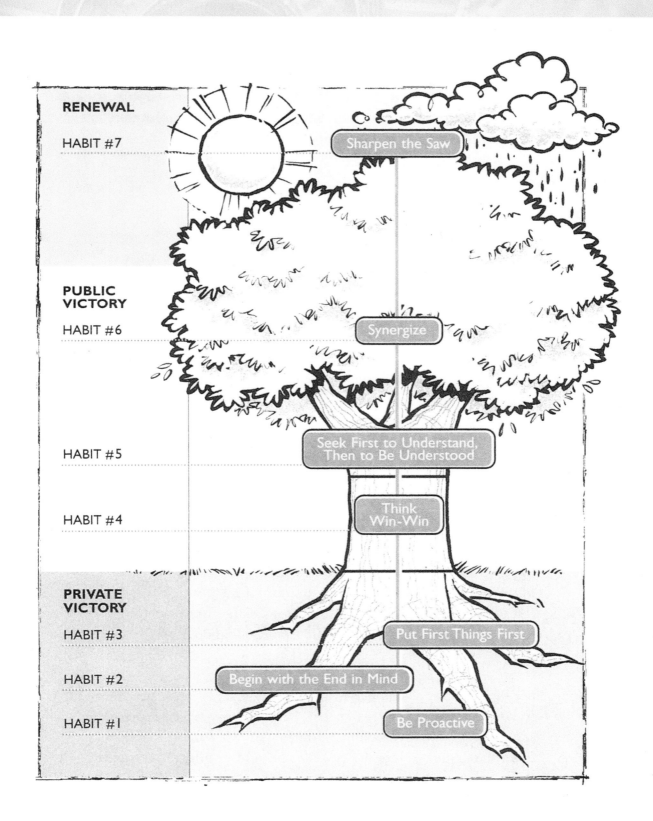

RENEWAL

HABIT #7 — Sharpen the Saw

PUBLIC VICTORY

HABIT #6 — Synergize

HABIT #5 — Seek First to Understand, Then to Be Understood

HABIT #4 — Think Win-Win

PRIVATE VICTORY

HABIT #3 — Put First Things First

HABIT #2 — Begin with the End in Mind

HABIT #1 — Be Proactive

The last habit, Habit 7, is the habit of renewal. It feeds all of the other six habits.

The habits seem rather simple, don't they? But just wait till you see how powerful they can be! One great way to understand what the 7 Habits are is to understand what they are not. So here are the opposites, or:

The 7 Habits of Highly Defective Teens

Habit 1: *React*

Blame all of your problems on your parents, your stupid teachers or professors, your lousy neighbourhood, your boy- or girlfriend, the government, or something or somebody else. Be a victim. Take no responsibility for your life. Act like an animal. If you're hungry, eat. If someone yells at you, yell back. If you feel like doing something you know is wrong, just do it.

Habit 2: *Begin with No End in Mind*

Don't have a plan. Avoid goals at all costs. And never think about tomorrow. Why worry about the consequences of your actions? Live for the moment. Sleep around, get wasted, and party on, for tomorrow we die.

Habit 3: *Put First Things Last*

Whatever is most important in your life, don't do it until you have spent sufficient time watching reruns, talking endlessly on the phone, surfing the Net, and lounging around. Always put off your homework until tomorrow. Make sure that things that don't matter always come before things that do.

Habit 4: *Think Win-Lose*

See life as a vicious competition. Your classmate is out to get you, so you'd better get him or her first. Don't let anyone else succeed at anything because, remember, if they win, you lose. If it looks like you're going to lose, however, make sure you drag that sucker down with you.

Habit 5: *Seek First to Talk, Then Pretend to Listen*

You were born with a mouth, so use it. Make sure you talk a lot. Always express your side of the story first. Once you're sure everyone understands your views, then pretend to listen by nodding and saying "uh-huh." Or, if you really want their opinion, give it to them.

Habit 6: *Don't Cooperate*

Let's face it, other people are weird because they're different from you. So why try to get along with them? Teamwork is for the dogs. Since you always have the best ideas, you are better off doing everything by yourself. Be your own island.

Habit 7: *Wear Yourself Out*

Be so busy with life that you never take time to renew or improve yourself. Never study. Don't learn anything new. Avoid exercise like the plague. And, for heaven's sake, stay away from good books, nature, or anything else that may inspire you.

As you can see, the habits listed above are recipes for disaster. Yet many of us indulge in them . . . regularly (me included). And, given this, it's no wonder that life can really stink at times.

What Exactly Are Habits?

Habits are things we do repeatedly. But most of the time we are hardly aware that we have them. They're on autopilot.

Some habits are good, such as:
• Exercising regularly
• Planning ahead
• Showing respect for others

Some are bad, like:
• Thinking negatively
• Feeling inferior
• Blaming others

And some don't really matter, including:
- Taking showers at night
- Eating yogurt with a fork
- Reading magazines from back to front

Depending on what they are, our habits will either make us or break us. We become what we repeatedly do. As writer Samuel Smiles put it:

> Sow a thought, and you reap an act;
> Sow an act, and you reap a habit;
> Sow a habit, and you reap a character;
> Sow a character, and you reap a destiny.

Luckily, you are stronger than your habits. Therefore, you can change them. For example, try folding your arms. Now try folding them in the opposite way. How does this feel? Pretty strange, doesn't it? But if you folded them in the opposite way for thirty days in a row, it wouldn't feel so strange. You wouldn't even have to think about it. You'd get in the habit.

At any time you can look yourself in the mirror and say, "Hey, I don't like that about myself," and you can exchange a bad habit for a better one. It's not always easy, but it's always possible.

Not every idea in this book will work for you. But you don't have to be perfect to see results, either. Just living some of the habits some of the time can help you experience changes in your life you never thought possible.

ACTIVITIES

DIRECTLY STATED IDEAS AND INFORMATION

1. According to the author, what is the first habit that highly effective teens should focus on?

2. What does the author mean by the phrase "Luckily, you are stronger than your habits"?

INDIRECTLY STATED IDEAS AND INFORMATION

3. Read the quotation from Samuel Smiles on page 24. Then find a sentence in the text that you think describes what Smiles is trying to say.

4. Look at the diagram of the tree. Explain why the first three habits are like the roots of a tree. Then, explain why the next three habits are like the trunk, branches, and leaves of the tree. Finally, explain why the seventh habit, renewal, is like the rain and sun.

MAKING CONNECTIONS

5. Draw a picture to illustrate the seven habits using another symbol that you think is appropriate. Explain why you chose this symbol.

WRITING EXTENSION

Summarize the seven habits of highly effective teens in your own words. Write one sentence for each of the habits.

A journey of a thousand miles
begins with a single step.

— *Chinese proverb*

READING STRATEGY

As you read this selection, remember to follow the numbering and read the rules in order.

VOCABULARY PREVIEW

- ingenuity
- personality conflict
- unceremoniously
- contradiction
- unique
- compassion

The 12 Rules About Hiring and Firing

❖ by Richard Bolles

1 Nobody owes you a job.

4 Your employers may lay you off, or fire you, anytime they want to. They may do this because they have run out of money, and can't afford you anymore. They may do this because they have to decrease the size of their business, or are going out of business. They may do this because they find your skills do not match the work that they need to have done. Or they may do this because they have a personality conflict with you.

6 Your employers may fire you, or lay you off, without any warning or much notice at all to you, dumping you unceremoniously out on the street.

8 If you are fired, your former employer may do everything in the world to help you find other employment, or may do nothing.

10 As you look back, you may feel that your employers treated you very well, in accordance with their stated values—or you may feel that your employers treated you very badly, in total contradiction of their stated values.

11 If you were the only one who was fired or let go, the other employees may promise they will fight to save your job, but you need to be prepared for the fact that when the chips are down, they may actually do nothing to help you. You will feel very alone.

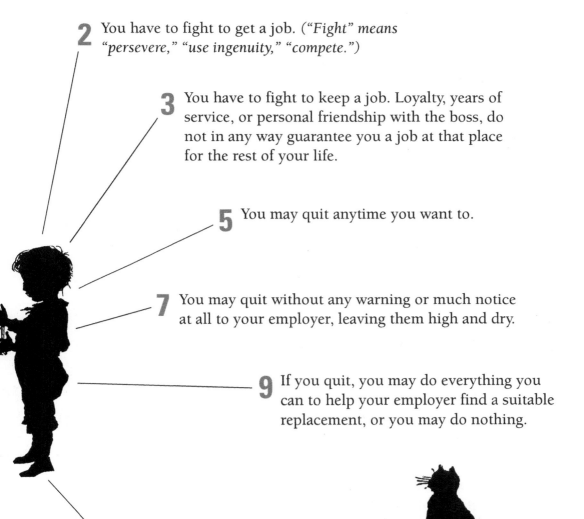

2 You have to fight to get a job. (*"Fight" means "persevere," "use ingenuity," "compete."*)

3 You have to fight to keep a job. Loyalty, years of service, or personal friendship with the boss, do not in any way guarantee you a job at that place for the rest of your life.

5 You may quit anytime you want to.

7 You may quit without any warning or much notice at all to your employer, leaving them high and dry.

9 If you quit, you may do everything you can to help your employer find a suitable replacement, or you may do nothing.

12 Nonetheless, you remain a rare and unique individual, no matter how the world of work treats you. Your worth is not defined simply by your work, but by your spirit, your heart, and your compassion toward others.

ACTIVITIES

DIRECTLY STATED IDEAS AND INFORMATION

1. Give one reason why your employer may lay you off or fire you.

2. What does "fight" mean in terms of getting a job? What does "fight" mean in terms of keeping your job?

INDIRECTLY STATED IDEAS AND INFORMATION

3. Look at the illustration. Why do you think the artist included a picture of a cat in the far right-hand corner? Which of the 12 rules is it meant to correspond to?

4. Rule 8 suggests that your employer may offer you real help in finding another job, or no help at all. Describe under what circumstances you might get no help, and under what circumstances you might hope for real help.

MAKING CONNECTIONS

5. Choose one of the 12 rules that you found interesting or surprising. Explain how knowing this rule might help you be better prepared for the workforce.

WRITING EXTENSION

Write an informative piece titled "Information for Employees and Employers About Hiring and Firing." Use the information in this text as the basis for your piece, but write it in your own words. Remember to connect ideas with transition words and phrases such as "on the other hand" or "in addition."

READING STRATEGY

*Before you read this article, **skim** it. To skim, read the title. Then look at any coloured headings, and read them. How do the headings connect to the title? What predictions can you make about the contents of the article?*

VOCABULARY PREVIEW

- exasperated
- dividends
- perceptive
- crucial
- inadvertently
- arrogant
- literally
- grating
- delve

Want to Do Better on the Job? Listen Up!

❖ by Diane Cole

When Linda S., an Ohio banking executive, learned she would not be promoted she asked her boss why. He had barely begun to speak when she blurted out, "I know that whatever the reason I can do better!"

Exasperated, he replied, "You always interrupt before you even know what I'm going to say! How can you do better if you never listen?"

"Most people value speaking—which is seen as active—over listening, which is seen as passive," explains Nancy Wyatt, professor of speech communication at Penn State University and co-author with Carol Ashburn of *Successful Listening* (Harper and Row, 1988).

And there are other reasons we might fail to tune in.

We may become so fixed on what we think that we tune out important information. Or we may react emotionally to a phrase or style the speaker uses and miss the main point. Or we're just too busy to pay attention to what is being said.

Sound familiar? If so, listen up, for changing your ways will pay big dividends. You'll stop wasting time on misunderstood assignments at work. People will start to see you as a perceptive, smart, and sensitive person who understands their needs. And that will open new opportunities on the job suggests Lyman K. Steil, Ph.D., president of Communication Development Inc., a consulting firm based in St. Paul, Minneapolis.

You can also develop an ear for the crucial but unspoken words in conversation that signal problems in your business relationships.

Here are some suggestions for learning to listen to what is said—and not said—more effectively.

Control distractions

Give a speaker your full attention or you're likely to miss the main point.

Identify the speaker's purpose

Tune in to the speaker's agenda. Is he or she there to let off steam, solve a problem, share information, or just schmooze? Once you know, you can respond in the way he or she wants and expects. Learning to listen may also keep you from inadvertently getting caught in the crossfire of office politics.

Don't finish other people's sentences

Many people have this bad habit. Just observe yourself: Do you cut people off before they finish a thought? Are you so busy thinking about what you want to say you can't resist breaking in?

"That often happens because the interrupter is bright, thinks she has grasped the point, and wants to show off how much she knows," says Dee Soder, Ph.D., president of Endymion, a New York City-based executive consulting firm. "What happens instead is that interrupters are perceived as being arrogant and interested only in themselves."

To break the habit of interruption, bite your tongue and follow up with your comments only after the other person has had his or her say. Soder suggests you might even have to literally sit on your hands to keep your gestures from speaking for you.

Finally, if you're not certain that the speaker has finished, ask!

Don't let the speaker's style turn you off

It's easy to tune out when less-than-favourite speakers clear their throats. One high school teacher confesses that for a long time she found a colleague's slow, deliberate drawl so grating that she simply could not listen to him. "It was only when I was forced to work with him and had to concentrate on *what* he was saying rather than how that I realized how smart and helpful he was and now we're best friends at work."

Don't be distracted by buzzwords

What springs to mind when you hear the label "feminist" or "right-to-lifer"? If you're like most people, emotions take over and you stop paying careful attention to the point a speaker is trying to make.

Listen for what is not being said

Sometimes it's important to "hear between the lines." "Many people like to avoid conflict and so the person speaking is very reluctant to say anything negative," says Soder.

When you suspect that a delicate or negative subject is being studiously avoided, you have to be prepared to delve deeper and ask the speaker, "Tell me more about that. Could you please explain?"

Show you are listening

Think about what your body language is revealing. Are you making good eye contact and leaning slightly forward in a way that indicates "I'm open to what you're saying"? Or are you tapping your foot and looking out the window as if to say, "I have more important things to do than listen to you"?

Make a note of it

Jotting down a word or two can remind you later of the main purpose behind the assignment your boss is giving you.

A brief note can also help you remember the point you would like to raise after the speaker finishes. For example, jot down "money" if you don't hear a potential employer mention it in an otherwise complete job description.

Make sure you heard it right

Many misunderstandings could be prevented if we'd just make sure we heard what we thought we heard. So when in doubt don't be afraid to ask, "Let me make sure I understand what you're saying." It's a hearing test well worth taking.

ACTIVITIES

DIRECTLY STATED IDEAS AND INFORMATION

1. According to the author, why do most people value speaking over listening?

2. According to the author, why do people finish other people's sentences?

INDIRECTLY STATED IDEAS AND INFORMATION

3. Why do "buzzwords" distract listeners from the meaning of the message?

4. How can speakers "read" their audience's reaction?

MAKING CONNECTIONS

5. Do the suggestions for better listening given in the text apply to other areas of life besides work life? Give specific examples to illustrate your point.

WRITING EXTENSION

Develop a pamphlet on better listening skills that could be handed out to new employees at a company. Decide on the layout of your pamphlet before you begin. Keep your points short, and think of ways to present the information in a friendly way (bullets, lists, graphics, etc.). Use ideas from your own experience or from the text, but express them in your own words.

READING STRATEGY

*Copy the **K-W-L chart** below into your notebook. Before you read, complete the first column by filling in things you know or think you know about the X Games. Fill in the second column with notes about what you would like to find out about the X Games.*

As you read, look for information to complete the third column with point-form answers to your questions. Where else could you look to find answers to your remaining questions?

What I KNOW	What I WANT to Know	What I Have LEARNED

VOCABULARY PREVIEW

- dominated
- aggressive
- arthroscopic
- stagnated
- excel
- piqued

The L.A. Times   Thursday, August 14, 2003

Fabiola da Silva's X-traordinary Career

❖ by Susan Carpenter

Think X Games and testosterone immediately comes to mind. The world of extreme sports is a world dominated by boys—boys racing over the edges of vert ramps on skateboards; boys performing airborne acrobatics on dirt bikes; boys skimming fast-moving waves on surfboards. Or so it seems.

There are a lot of girls too, but they don't get nearly as much attention. Take aggressive in-line skater Fabiola da Silva. With six golds to her credit, she's the most medalled female athlete at the X Games, taking place for the ninth time this weekend at L.A.'s Staples Center. She's also the only girl to compete against boys in any X Games sport—aggressive in-line vert—yet few people outside of the extreme sports world even know her name.

Does da Silva care? No. The 24-year-old Brazilian is gender blind.

"A lot of girls think girls aren't good enough to be skating against the guys," she explained in English with a slight Brazilian accent. "I just think different. If I see a guy doing it, I think it's possible for a woman to do it also. Why not?"

Known to fans as "Fabby," da Silva packs a lot of punch into her 5-foot-2-inch, 112-pound frame. She has a reputation for skating harder, faster, and more fearlessly than any of her female peers, so much so that in 2002 the Aggressive Skaters Association discontinued its women's vert competitions because "there was just no depth of talent beyond Fabiola," said ASA Executive Director Todd Shays.

"She's strong, she's gutsy, and she's willing to try," he said. "You have to really have guts on the half pipe because if you fall, it's a long way down."

How far down? About 18 feet if you glide up to the top of a 13-foot half pipe, then catch 5 feet of air over its edge to do a major trick.

Da Silva has, unfortunately, been there. One week before last year's X Games she lost her footing while grinding the undersides of her skates along the top of the ramp. She flipped over and landed on the flat bottom, twisting her knee so badly she needed arthroscopic surgery.

Such an accident might have stopped a lesser skater, but not da Silva.

In preparation for this year's games, she's been working out for two hours, then skating an additional four or five hours each day. The only female in a field of 35, she's expected to place in the top 10 this weekend.

Between 1996, when she first started competing in the X Games, and 2001, the last year there was a vert division for women, da Silva placed first every year except 1999, when she was defeated by Japanese skater Ayumi Kawasaki and placed second.

"Fabiola progressed enormously early on in her career, and then kind of stagnated when there was a separate women's division and there was no one pushing her. She was just winning," said Shays. "It was exciting in 2002 when we combined the men and women to see her level shoot up again. She was skating with and against skaters who are much better than her, and it pushed her to excel."

Da Silva has been in-line skating for a decade, beginning in Sao Paulo, Brazil, where she was born. At age 12, she started skateboarding just to have fun with her friends, "but then I saw some guys roller-blading."

Her interest was piqued. She dug out the pair of roller skates she had at home to try it out, decided she liked it, and quickly made the move to Rollerblades. Five years ago she moved to California. She now lives in Santa Ana.

"It's closer to the skate parks," she said. In her native Brazil, da Silva skated only on the street, but "when I moved to America everybody was doing everything, so I started skating everything," she said. "I think it helps you to become a better skater."

These days da Silva still skates street. In this weekend's aggressive in-line street competition, which still has a women's field, she's expected to medal. But she excels in vert because it's her passion.

"It feels so good to be able to skate big ramps," she said.

Of the events showcased at the X Games, aggressive in-line skating may not be as well known as skateboarding or BMX biking, but it's a sport that continues to grow in popularity. The National Sporting Goods Association estimates there are 28 million in-line skaters internationally, with aggressive skating the fastest-growing segment of the market.

Like mountain boarding, sand boarding, and other up-and-coming extreme sports, aggressive in-line skating is heavily influenced by skateboarding. It surfaced in the early 80s, when in-line skates, formerly an off-season training device for hockey players, crossed over to the general public as Rollerblades.

It was 1981 when a handful of bladers started riding their in-line skates on the same terrain as skateboarders, performing copycat tricks on rails and ramps.

Not surprisingly, the Rollerblade brand has a lock on the aggressive in-line skate market. It is also one of the handful of sponsors that allow da Silva to do her thing full time.

"The reason I am in the U.S.A. is for skating," she said. "Roller-blading is my life." ■

ACTIVITIES

DIRECTLY STATED IDEAS AND INFORMATION

1. In which sport is Fabiola the only female competing against males?

2. List three sports that are part of the X Games.

INDIRECTLY STATED IDEAS AND INFORMATION

3. Why did the Aggressive Skaters Association discontinue its women's vert competitions in 2002?

4. Why did Fabiola start to improve as a skater once she started competing with men?

MAKING CONNECTIONS

5. Explain why you think the world of extreme sports is dominated by males.

WRITING EXTENSION

Write a well-developed opinion piece that answers the question "Should women be allowed to compete against men in sports?" Make sure you pre-plan your writing using a T-chart. You should have a minimum of three paragraphs.

READING STRATEGY

Scanning is a useful strategy for a schedule like this one. To scan, run your eyes quickly over the words, looking for specific information. In this case, you could look for all the occurrences of the key phrase "aggressive in-line vert." This information will be useful when you are answering the first two questions.

VOCABULARY PREVIEW

- aggressive
- vert
- jam
- prelim
- wakeboard
- freestyle

X Games IX Schedules

Address: http://www.expn.com

LOS ANGELES

X GAMES IX, LOS ANGELES, AUGUST 14 - 17, 2003

EXPN IX

HOME
EVENT SCHEDULE
TV SCHEDULE
RESULTS
QUALIFIED RIDERS
SPONSORS
EXPN PRO SHOP
THE MUSIC OF X
X GAMES SKATEPARKS

X Games IX Event Schedule
Los Angeles, CA — Western Time

	Time	Venue
Friday, August 15, 2003 *EXPN Central Schedule*		
Aggressive In-Line Vert Practice	8:30 AM – 12:30 PM	STAPLES Center
Moto X Step Up Practice	10:30 AM – 12:30 PM	STAPLES Center
Skateboard Park Women's Practice	11:30 AM – 12:30 PM	STAPLES Center
Bike Stunt Flatland Practice	11:30 AM – 1:30 PM	STAPLES Center
Skateboard Park **Women's Jam**	12:30 PM – 1:30 PM	STAPLES Center

X Games Raw
Live, un-cut, exclusive video straight from X Games IX.

Video Highlights
The best of X Games past and present.

Photo Galleries
Exclusive snaps from X Games IX.

Chat Series
Now you can talk with the X Games elite.

Kagy Collection
Life through a digital camera in the hands of Chad Kagy.

Tags
What's your signature on the world?

Address: http://www.expn.com

HOME
EVENT SCHEDULE
TV SCHEDULE
RESULTS
QUALIFIED RIDERS
SPONSORS
EXPN PRO SHOP
THE MUSIC OF X
X GAMES SKATEPARKS

X Games IX Event Schedule
Los Angeles, CA — Western Time

	Time	Venue
Moto X Step Up **Final**	12:30 PM – 2:30 PM	STAPLES Center
Bike Stunt Flatland **Final**	1:30 PM – 2:30 PM	STAPLES Center
Bike Stunt Vert Practice	2:30 PM – 3:30 PM	STAPLES Center
Bike Stunt Park Practice	2:30 PM – 6:00 PM	STAPLES Center
Skateboard Park Men's Practice	2:30 PM – 6:00 PM	STAPLES Center
Bike Stunt Vert Prelims	3:30 PM – 6:00 PM	STAPLES Center
Skateboard Vert Practice	6:00 PM – 7:30 PM	STAPLES Center
Skateboard Vert **Final**	7:30 PM – 9:00 PM	STAPLES Center

Saturday, August 16, 2003
EXPN Central Schedule

Aggressive In-Line Vert Practice	9:00 AM – 11:00 AM	STAPLES Center
Bike Stunt Park Practice	10:00 AM – 1:00 PM	STAPLES Center
Skateboard Park Practice	10:00 AM – 1:00 PM	STAPLES Center
Aggressive In-Line Vert Prelims	11:00 AM – 1:30 PM	STAPLES Center
Wakeboard Men's & Women's Practice	12:00 PM – 3:30 PM	Long Beach
Bike Stunt Park **Final**	1:00 PM – 3:30 PM	STAPLES Center
Skateboard Vert Doubles Practice	1:30 PM – 3:30 PM	STAPLES Center
Moto X Freestyle Practice	2:00 PM – 6:00 PM	L.A. Coliseum
Skateboard Vert Doubles **Final**	3:30 PM – 5:30 PM	STAPLES Center
Moto X Freestyle Prelims	6:00 PM – 7:30 PM	L.A. Coliseum

X Games Raw
Live, un-cut, exclusive video straight from X Games IX.

Video Highlights
The best of X Games past and present.

Photo Galleries
Exclusive snaps from X Games IX.

Chat Series
Now you can talk with the X Games elite.

Kagy Collection
Life through a digital camera in the hands of Chad Kagy.

Tags
What's your signature on the world?

Address: http://www.expn.com

EXPN

HOME
EVENT SCHEDULE
TV SCHEDULE
RESULTS
QUALIFIED RIDERS
SPONSORS
EXPN PRO SHOP
THE MUSIC OF X
X GAMES SKATEPARKS

X Games IX Event Schedule
Los Angeles, CA — Western Time

	Time	Venue
Moto X Freestyle Practice	7:30 PM – 8:00 PM	L.A. Coliseum
Moto X Freestyle **Final**	8:00 PM – 9:00 PM	L.A. Coliseum
Sunday, August 17, 2003 *EXPN Central Schedule*		
Moto X Big Air Practice	9:00 AM – 11:00 AM	STAPLES Center
Skateboard Vert Best Trick Practice	10:00 AM – 11:30 AM	STAPLES Center
Skateboard Park Practice	10:00 AM – 1:00 PM	STAPLES Center
Wakeboard Men's and Women's Practice	11:00 AM – 1:00 PM	Long Beach
Skateboard Vert Best Trick **Final**	11:30 AM – 12:30 PM	STAPLES Center
Aggressive In-Line Vert Practice	12:30 PM – 1:30 PM	STAPLES Center
Skateboard Park **Final**	1:00 PM – 3:30 PM	STAPLES Center
Wakeboard Men's Prelims	1:00 PM – 2:30 PM	Long Beach
Aggressive In-Line Vert **Final**	1:30 PM – 2:30 PM	STAPLES Center
Bike Stunt Vert Practice	2:30 PM – 4:00 PM	STAPLES Center
Wakeboard Women's **Final**	2:30 PM – 3:15 PM	Long Beach
Wakeboard Men's **Final**	3:15 PM – 4:00 PM	Long Beach
Bike Stunt Vert **Final**	4:00 PM – 6:00 PM	STAPLES Center
Skateboard Vert **Women's Demo**	6:00 PM – 6:45 PM	STAPLES Center
Moto X Big Air Practice	6:00 PM – 7:00 PM	STAPLES Center
Moto X Big Air **Final**	7:00 PM – 9:00 PM	STAPLES Center

X Games Raw
Live, un-cut, exclusive video straight from X Games IX.

Video Highlights
The best of X Games past and present.

Photo Galleries
Exclusive snaps from X Games IX.

Chat Series
Now you can talk with the X Games elite.

Kagy Collection
Life through a digital camera in the hands of Chad Kagy.

Tags
What's your signature on the world?

Games IX
LOS ANGELES
X GAMES IX, LOS ANGELES, AUGUST 14 - 17, 2003

EXPN

HOME
EVENT SCHEDULE
TV SCHEDULE
RESULTS
QUALIFIED RIDERS
SPONSORS
EXPN PRO SHOP
THE MUSIC OF X
X GAMES SKATEPARKS

X Games IX TV Schedule
Los Angeles, CA — Western Time

	Time	Channel
Saturday, August 16, 2003		
Bike Stunt Dirt, Bike Stunt Vert, Moto X Step Up Final, Skateboard Street Final, Skateboard Vert	2 pm ET/3 pm PT	ABC
Sunday, August 17, 2003		
Bike Stunt Dirt Final, Bike Stunt Park Final, Moto X Freestyle, Skateboard Vert Final	4 pm	ABC
Bike Stunt Vert Final (LIVE), Moto X Freestyle Final, Skateboard Vert Doubles Final	7 pm ET/7 pm PT	ABC
Monday, August 18, 2003		
Aggressive In-Line Vert Final, Bike Stunt Flatland Final, Skateboard Street Best Trick Final	5 pm ET	ESPN
Aggressive In-Line Vert Final, Downhill BMX, Wakeboard Men's Final	9 – 11 pm ET	ESPN2
Tuesday, August 19, 2003		
Men's & Women's Aggressive In-Line Park Final, Wakeboard Women's Final	5 – 6 pm ET	ESPN
Downhill BMX Final, Moto X Big Air, Skateboard Park Final, Surfing	9 – 11 pm ET	ESPN2
Wednesday, August 20, 2003		
Moto X Big Air, Skateboard Vert Best Trick Final, Surfing	9 – 11 pm ET	ESPN
Thursday, August 21, 2003		
Moto X Big Air Final, Surfing Final	9 – 10 pm ET	ESPN

X Games Raw
Live, un-cut, exclusive video straight from X Games IX.

Video Highlights
The best of X Games past and present.

Photo Galleries
Exclusive snaps from X Games IX.

Chat Series
Now you can talk with the X Games elite.

Kagy Collection
Life through a digital camera in the hands of Chad Kagy.

Tags
What's your signature on the world?

ACTIVITIES

DIRECTLY STATED IDEAS AND INFORMATION

1. When and where was the final for the aggressive in-line vert competition held? What day and times was it broadcast?

2. What link would you follow to find out who won the aggressive in-line vert competition?

INDIRECTLY STATED IDEAS AND INFORMATION

3. Explain why the event schedule is longer than the TV schedule.

4. Explain why some words are in boldface in the event schedule.

MAKING CONNECTIONS

5. Why do you think they are called the X Games?

WRITING EXTENSION

Write a news report dated Monday, August 4, 2003 with the headline "X Games Set to Begin." Use information from the Event Schedule and the TV Schedule in your report. Also include a quotation from an athlete or official at the games (you can make this part up).

READING STRATEGY

*Sammy Sosa did not become successful all at once. A series of events led to his success. Copy the following **event map** into your notebook, and as you read this story, complete the map (the first one has been done for you):*

Event 1: Sammy's father died when he was 6.
Event 2: _____
Event 3: _____
Event 4: _____
Event 5: _____

Sammy Sosa

"My biggest mistake was trading Sammy Sosa."

— President George W. Bush, who formerly owned Sammy's first baseball team, the Texas Rangers

Sammy burst into the kitchen, grinning from ear to ear. His mother was at the stove, fanning herself to keep cool in the muggy heat. He glanced around at his six brothers and sisters crammed into a single room and thought, *I hate this place.* The tin roof, the dirt floor, the smell of garbage . . . for years he had dreamed of buying his family a nice, big, clean house to live in. And three huge meals a day to fill their bellies.

"Mama," he said quietly, holding a piece of paper out to her, "we're millionaires." She took the cheque from his hand and stared at it for the longest time, as tears began streaming down her face. For the Sosa family, it might as well have been a million dollars. The cheque was for over three thousand dollars—more than Sammy's mother could earn in years of working as a maid. *Maybe God has finally heard my prayers*, she thought. Maybe indeed. Her son, Sammy Sosa, had just signed his first pro ball contract . . . and he was just 16 years old!

This future baseball legend was born in the Dominican Republic, an island nation in the Caribbean. Sammy's father drove a tractor in the sugarcane fields that cover the island, and his mother cleaned the houses of the wealthy. Sammy was just six when his father died suddenly from cancer, changing his world overnight.

With eight mouths to feed, everyone in the family had to work. Sammy left home in the dark early mornings to shine shoes, went to school during the day, spent evenings washing cars, and returned home long after the sun set. He gave every penny he earned to his mother, but many nights the family still went to bed hungry. These hard times changed Sammy forever:

> When you don't have any control over your economic situation, when your stomach is empty, when you see your mother working so hard . . . it leaves a mark on you.

He vowed he would pull himself and his family out of poverty one day.

When the family moved from their small village to a larger city, things got even worse. The eight of them crowded into a one-bedroom shack with dirt floors and no indoor plumbing. The streets were covered in trash and raw sewage. Sammy worked hard shining shoes. One customer, American businessman Bill Chase, was so impressed with Sammy and his brothers' hard work that he hired them to sweep the floors of his factory. Sammy got paid about $20 a week—a huge improvement on his shoe-shining money. At 13, he knew his mother had no money for college, and he didn't have time to take this job and go to classes, so he quit school.

Although he was sad to quit school, the decision had one good outcome: more time to play baseball! Baseball is the national sport of the Dominican Republic. "In my country small boys begin playing baseball not long after they learn to walk." Sammy hadn't played much as a kid, he was too busy working, but when Bill heard he was learning to play, he bought Sammy his first baseball glove.

Now he had a focus: He knew that some Dominicans got into the major leagues and that there was money to be made . . . but only if he was great. He talked Bill into giving his other brothers extra hours sweeping so that he could devote more time to practice. "For me there weren't any days off," remembered Sammy. "I worked at baseball every day." He played in the streets and dirt lots, using sticks for bats and balled-up rags, stuffed corn husks, and even old milk cartons for baseballs.

Although he started playing baseball later than most Dominican kids, Sammy worked harder than anyone else. After just a year of playing, the 14-year-old was attracting crowds, and even television cameras, to his games. When jealous players said he was crazy to dream of playing in the major leagues, Sammy ignored them and worked even harder.

He auditioned for tons of major league scouts, but got rejected again and again. "You're not fast enough," "You're not strong enough," "You're not big enough," they said. But Sammy didn't give up. The next year, when he turned 16, scouts for the Texas Rangers watched him play and invited Sammy to join the team. That's when they gave him the $3500 cheque—a signing bonus (almost three times his yearly salary), which he gave to his mother, of course. It was his dream come true.

Sammy's whole family went to the airport that day in 1986 when he left for the United States. He was both excited and terrified, and not just because it was his first time in an airplane. Sammy knew he still faced an uphill battle once he reached the U.S. Ninety to ninety-five percent of foreign-born baseball players get sent home after starting in the major leagues. Would he be one of the unlucky majority? Sammy spent years working his way up through the minor leagues, struggling to learn the game and build his strength (eating a more

nutritious diet, he bulked up from a skinny 160 pounds to a hulking 210 pounds). All the while he sent every penny of his small salary back home to his family.

But Sammy never got sent home. In 1989, after proving himself in the minor leagues, he was finally invited to play in the major league games. He surprised the whole league with his talent early in the season when he hit a home run against Roger Clemens, one of the best pitchers of all time. It was his first major league home run, but it certainly wouldn't be his last. Sammy was a spotty player at first and was traded several times, first to the Chicago White Sox and then to the Chicago Cubs. But over the years his playing steadily improved. In 1993 he became the first Cub in history to hit 33 home runs and steal 30 bases in a single season. Only a few of the greatest players of all time had done that!

With the Cubs, Sammy's fame grew, but it wasn't until 1998 that his name became a household word. He and Mark McGuire of the St. Louis Cardinals were neck-and-neck to break Roger Maris's record of 61 home runs in a single season, set in 1961. McGuire was the first to break it in a game against the Cubs, and Sammy proved his generous nature by running in from right field to hug and congratulate McGuire. But just when everyone thought the race was over, Sammy broke Maris's record as well. He was happy to share the glory with McGuire, saying, "He's *the man* in the United States and I am *the man* in the

Dominican Republic." In the end, Sammy hit 66 home runs to McGuire's 70, and was voted Most Valuable Player in both the National League and on the all-star team. He even made the cover of *Sports Illustrated* as Sportsman of the Year.

Sammy was not only a baseball hero, but one of its highest-paid players as well, earning over $10 million a year. He was able to buy his family a new house, and his mother never had to work again. The Dominican Republic named him "Ambassador of Baseball," and even President Bill Clinton honoured him in the 1998 State of the Union Address and invited him to the White House to light the national Christmas tree.

Just as he assisted his family, Sammy wanted to help the country he loves. He boosted tourism in the Dominican Republic by starring in commercials encouraging people to travel there. He established a foundation to support needy Dominican families and a medical centre to give free medical care to their children. Each year Dominican schools receive more than $500 000 from Sammy, and 40 computers for every home run he hits! When a devastating hurricane wiped out many Caribbean communities, Sammy created a fund to get victims back on their feet.

I want to be known as a good person more than a good baseball player. I am prouder of my rebuilding efforts than all of my home runs. I love my country. I will do anything I can to help them.

He also helps out in the United States. His "Sammy Claus World Tour" gives away toys to over 7000 children. And baseball Sundays at Wrigley Field are now called "Sammy Days" because he donates tickets to low-income kids. In 1998, Sammy was honoured for his generosity with the Gene Autry Courage Award for athletes who "demonstrate heroism in the face of adversity and overcome hardships to inspire others."

Sammy's story inspires people in America and around the world. They see that America has embraced this outsider— a black, Spanish-speaking man from the Dominican Republic—as one of its heroes. Sammy has led a movement in baseball towards accepting Latino players, who now make up more than 25 percent of U.S. teams. But with all his money and fame, Sammy never forgets where he came from. While most major league players practise in state-of-the-art gyms and pristine baseball diamonds, Sammy still practises in his old dirt ball field in the Dominican Republic. Surrounded by the sights, sounds, and people he grew up with, he can remember the struggles of his childhood, the lessons he has learned, and can see how far he's come. ■

ACTIVITIES

DIRECTLY STATED IDEAS AND INFORMATION

1. What happened to Sammy's father?

2. What was the first team Sammy played for in the U.S.?

INDIRECTLY STATED IDEAS AND INFORMATION

3. Explain why the phrase "Maybe God has finally heard my prayers" is written in italics (paragraph 2).

4. Explain why Sammy still practises on the old dirt ball field in the Dominican Republic.

MAKING CONNECTIONS

5. Explain whether you believe Sammy's success is due to talent or hard work. Use information from the reading selection and your own ideas to support your opinion.

WRITING EXTENSION

Based on what you have read and your own ideas, write an opinion piece on whether you feel professional athletes like Sammy Sosa are overpaid. State your opinion near the beginning, and include at least two arguments with supporting details to back up your opinion. End with a few sentences that summarize your point of view.

You miss 100% of the shots you never take.

— *Wayne Gretzky (b. 1961)*
Athlete

READING STRATEGY

Before you answer the questions on the following page, look down the left-hand column of the chart. How is the information organized? Then look across the top row (in green). To find out what each of the letter abbreviations means, check the glossary on the following page.

VOCABULARY
PREVIEW

◆ average

◆ percentage

◆ glossary

◆ slugging

◆ strikeout

Sammy Sosa: Batting Statistics

YEAR	TEAM	G	AB	R	H	HR	RBI	BB	SO	SB	CS	OBP	SLG	AVG
1989	TEX-CHW	58	183	27	47	4	13	11	47	7	5	.303	.366	.257
1990	CHW	153	532	72	124	15	70	33	150	32	16	.282	.404	.233
1991	CHW	116	316	39	64	10	33	14	98	13	6	.240	.335	.203
1992	CHC	67	262	41	68	8	25	19	63	15	7	.317	.393	.260
1993	CHC	159	598	92	156	33	93	38	135	36	11	.309	.485	.261
1994	CHC	105	426	59	128	25	70	25	92	22	13	.339	.545	.300
1995	CHC	144	564	89	151	36	119	58	134	34	7	.340	.500	.268
1996	CHC	124	498	84	136	40	100	34	134	18	5	.323	.564	.273
1997	CHC	162	642	90	161	36	119	45	174	22	12	.300	.480	.251
1998	CHC	159	643	134	198	66	158	73	171	18	9	.377	.647	.308
1999	CHC	162	625	114	180	63	141	78	171	7	8	.367	.635	.288
2000	CHC	156	604	106	193	50	138	91	168	7	4	.406	.634	.320
2001	CHC	160	577	146	189	64	160	116	153	0	2	.437	.737	.328
2002	CHC	150	556	122	160	49	108	103	144	2	0	.399	.594	.288
2003	CHC	137	517	99	144	40	103	62	143	0	1	.358	.553	.279
TOTAL		2012	7543	1314	2099	539	1450	800	1977	233	106	.349	.546	.278

GLOSSARY

AB	*at bat*	**OBP**	*on-base percentage*
AVG	*batting average*	**R**	*runs*
BB	*bases on balls or walks*	**RBI**	*runs batted in*
CS	*caught stealing*	**SB**	*stolen bases*
G	*games*	**SLG**	*slugging percentage*
H	*hits*	**SO**	*strikeouts*
HR	*homeruns*		

ACTIVITIES

DIRECTLY STATED IDEAS AND INFORMATION

1. Use the glossary to find out which column lists Sammy Sosa's batting average. Then, look down the column to find out what year he had his highest batting average.

2. Look at the glossary again. Which column lists the number of home runs he hit each year? What year did he hit the most home runs?

INDIRECTLY STATED IDEAS AND INFORMATION

3. Explain why your answers to questions 1 and 2 are not the same.

4. According to these statistics and your own ideas, explain whether Sammy Sosa is at the peak of his career, is still improving each year, or is declining.

MAKING CONNECTIONS

5. Look in a newspaper or on the Internet to find statistics for another professional baseball player. Compare this player's home runs, stolen bases, and runs batted in statistics with Sosa's. Write three sentences that summarize what you found out in your comparison.

WRITING EXTENSION

Write an information paragraph that outlines Sammy Sosa's batting career through the years as provided by these statistics. Use complete sentences and link your ideas using time words such as "then," "later," or "now."

READING STRATEGY

As you read through this selection, write down three points that the author uses to prove the statement "Kids are stereotyped by shopkeepers." These notes will be helpful when you are completing the writing activity.

VOCABULARY PREVIEW

- ◆ stereotyped
- ◆ intentions
- ◆ suspiciously
- ◆ independence
- ◆ shunned

Editorial, *The Globe and Mail*   July 22, 2003

Kids Are the Forgotten Consumers

❖ by Zoe Anderson-Jenkins

Kids are stereotyped by shopkeepers as little thieves with no money, and with only the worst of intentions.

This, now, is coming from a kid: Trust me, they couldn't be more wrong.

Kids have money to spend. That is something that most adults misunderstand. I'm a teenage girl living in Toronto. I receive a monthly allowance of $80. With my money, I am expected to buy lunch for myself once a week, and subway tickets to get to school. With the remainder, I may do what I please.

The fact is that kids are consumers. When we walk into a store and are completely ignored, we will find somewhere else to spend our money. We will spend our money where we are respected, so should it not be in the best interests of the shop owners to treat us with respect?

Kids are usually ignored or hassled by shop owners. For example, I was recently in a convenience store in the CBC's headquarters in downtown Toronto. I was with my mom, but she was looking at magazines on the other side of the store when I was trying to pay for my bubble gum. Since I looked like I was on my own, the shopkeeper thought that it was okay to completely ignore me. I stood waiting for what seemed like an hour while four adults were served before me. I would have stood there all day until a woman in her late forties, who actually gave me the time of day, stopped the storekeeper, and said, pointing at me: "Excuse me, but I believe that she was first."

The shopkeeper, immediately assuming that she was my mother, plastered his face with a fake grin, and, eyeing the money in my hand, sold me my gum.

Some store owners don't ignore kids, they just watch them suspiciously, assuming they will steal or cause trouble.

I was in a store that sold makeup, waiting for my mom to buy some of her usual expensive perfume; three eager sales ladies were ready and willing to serve her. I was trying on lip gloss nearby. The sales ladies, rather than coming over to help me, began peeking suspiciously around boxes of merchandise, watching me. As soon as I had finished, two sales ladies rushed over and sprayed the tester station with what seemed to be disinfectant, while checking the stock around the booth, making sure that nothing had been taken or damaged.

Sadly, it's not just storekeepers who are rude to kids. It's many adults. Some teachers ignore kids. When I was younger, I had a teacher who did this frequently. While asking her for homework help, in mid-sentence she would cut me off, to engage in a 10-minute conversation with another teacher or a visiting parent.

When kids are small, shopping with their mothers, storekeepers treat them as if they are little angels, giving them candies and tons of attention. This attention is totally fake and put on to attract business from the mother. As soon as those kids get money of their own, and begin gaining independence, it's those same stores whose owners and salespeople are rude and disrespectful to them. The shopkeepers automatically assume: No mother, no money, no business.

Sadly, not only are they wrong, but they will lose a lot of business with that kind of thinking.

Many adults think that kids have no rights, money, or the capability of defending themselves by talking back. That is not so. Most kids don't steal, most kids will talk back, in defence of themselves, and most kids do have money to spend. If we have the same rights as all adults do, then why are we so often treated as second-class citizens?

Stereotyping is the basis for all forms of racism. The way some adults stereotype kids is just as bad, and even has its own name: ageism. Millions of kids in North America experience it every day, yet no one seems to think that ageism to kids is even a problem.

I have a friend my age who is black. When I go into a certain convenience store with her, the clerk makes her wait outside, telling her that she touches too many things, and that she will steal. I know my friend, and I know that she would never steal, has never stolen, yet the woman in the store automatically thinks this. The store clerk is simply racist, yet I wonder what it must be like for my friend to live through two types of discrimination.

Kids have good memories. The shops and places that are not rude to kids are the places that will get our business. When we are older, with more money to spend, and more things we need to buy, why would we want to shop in a place that once shunned us for being young?

While adults are the consumers of today, we are the consumers of tomorrow. ■

ACTIVITIES

DIRECTLY STATED IDEAS AND INFORMATION

1. Find a word that means that kids are discriminated against because of their age. Write down that word.

2. The author states that it is not only storekeepers who are rude to kids. What other group of adults does she specifically identify?

INDIRECTLY STATED IDEAS AND INFORMATION

3. Why was the shopkeeper nicer to the author once he thought the older woman was her mother?

4. Explain what is meant by the statement "we are the consumers of tomorrow" in the concluding sentence.

MAKING CONNECTIONS

5. Explain whether you think "Kids are the Forgotten Consumers" is a good title for this piece. Suggest an alternative.

WRITING EXTENSION

Write a 15-word summary of this reading selection. Make sure you include an introductory statement that contains a clear main idea and at least three supporting details.

READING STRATEGY

Copy the following **story frame** into your notebook. As you are reading, keep the story frame in mind, and when you finish reading the selection, go back and fill it in.

In this story, the problem starts when . . .
After that . . .
Next . . .
Then . . .
The problem is finally solved when . . .
The story ends with . . .

How did this activity help you to read the story?

VOCABULARY PREVIEW

- impression
- unidentifiable
- patronize
- unusual
- decorated
- grateful

The Tiniest Guitar in the World

❖ by Martha Brooks

I am following Fletcher P. (Flint) Eastwood down the hall. I've been ordered to his office, where we will sit and the lid on his good eye will jump up and down like a butterfly in a frenzy before he'll calmly ask, "What's up, Petrie?"

I will respond politely, "Nothing, *sir*," because my father went to an army academy and he taught me that this always makes a good impression. It also drives Mr. Eastwood crazy. The way I say *sir*, he can't find any fault with.

He's built like a retired football player and sort of bounces when he walks. His suits—all three of them—fit too tight in the jacket and too loose in the pants. There's a little ring of blondish grey hair that sits on his ears like a costume store bald wig, and the skin on top is firebrick red. Which is why we call him Flint.

His dinky office smells of eraser crumbs and old coffee and unidentifiable aftershave. You might say it's like a second home to me.

We get inside. He closes the door. "Sit," he says to the orange chair in front of his desk.

I sit down and kick at a paper ball near my feet. Beside it is a paper clip. I pick that up so I'll have something to fiddle with.

Flint settles in behind the desk, sighs, wipes his face with a wrinkly hand. I shoot a look at him in time to catch the butterfly-in-a-frenzy eyelid manoeuvre. His chair makes that old familiar squeak as he leans dangerously far back. He pauses, then comes forward fast. His elbows hit the desktop with a hollow sound like distant drums.

"What's up, Petrie?"

I've twisted the paper clip so that it's like a square with half the top missing. "Nothing, *sir*."

"Goddamn it, Donald—don't patronize me. Mrs. Lindblad *saw* you outside at noon."

"What? Sir?"

"You and your friends. Robert Isles and that . . . Goran fellow—Chris. Loose brown cigarette papers. Does that ring a bell?"

"Loose *brown* cigarette papers?"

He leans in on me. "Are you boys selling drugs?"

The paper clip now resembles a mutilated snake.

"Put that thing down and answer me."

I toss the clip. It bounces off the desk leg and veers back, tangling itself into the laces of my boot. "No, sir," I mumble, pulling it off.

The worst thing about somebody making up their mind that you're a liar is that you can tell the truth until you're blue in the face, but they aren't going to believe you, anyway.

"What's that? What did you say?" He's practically lying on his desk.

"I said, no, sir."

"Dammit, look at me when you answer."

I look. The other eye is glass. The colour doesn't quite match his good eye.

"No . . . sir."

"You know, Donald, I can't think of a single other person in this school who spends more time in this office, but it never seems to faze you."

He talks to me a lot about stuff not fazing me—my poor grades, my total disregard for the school's dress code, and my being a disturbing influence.

"You were *seen*, Donald. Outside, at *noon. Rolling marijuana cigarettes and selling them to the seventh-grade boys!*"

At noon. Outside at noon. Robert Isles, Chris Goran, and I found a dead squirrel. It was flattened—fairly fresh roadkill. Its mouth was open, its teeth bared. Its right arm stretched up past its ear. The other hung down around its belly. Goran starts joking around that it's lip synching. Isles is sucking on a can of root beer. Goran holds up the squirrel. Makes its left paw twitch frantically up and down. Isles spews root beer all over the ground. And that's when I get this unusual idea.

Goran's little brother, Paul, walks by with Simon Wiebe. We make them go into their classroom and bring out a pair of scissors. And what happens next is pretty amazing. Everybody hangs around watching. It's about the most creative thing I've done since I was a little kid.

"Donald, I've given you more warnings and second chances than just about anyone in the history of this school," Flint says, fishing around his shirt pocket under his grey pinstriped suit jacket. He pulls out a fresh pack of gum. "What is it you care about?" He picks at the outside wrapper. "I'd really like to know." He can't get the tab undone. He finally mangles it open and offers me a stick.

"No, thanks, sir. It's bad for my teeth."

Patiently smiling, he takes a piece of gum for himself. He's going to act all buddy-buddy now. This is the ace up his sleeve, as they say. Sometimes you go to see the vice-principal or a counsellor or whatever because you really need help. I don't know if they think you *enjoy* asking for help, or what. But you're depressed. They offer you a piece of gum. You tell them your problems because who else have you got to turn to—your mother? Then they offer you some turd piece of advice that messes you up even more because on top of everything else, you now have to worry about this new evidence they have on you, and about how they'll use it against you whenever they're in the right mood and you're in the wrong place.

So much for the buddy system.

Flint leans his arm on the desk, his chin on the palm of his hairy hand. It's his I'm-open-to-anything-you-have-to-tell-me-because-I'm-a-reasonable-caring-human-being position.

"Have you given any further thought to what you might do after you leave school?"

He's leading up to my becoming a drug dealer. Or to washing dishes at Mr. Steak for the rest of my life.

"Well, sir, lately I've been thinking seriously about marine biology."

"I see." He chews away. Waits for me to continue. We've been over this ground before.

"I worry about oil spills. Stuff like that."

"Stuff . . . like . . . that," he repeats, drawing out my words like my life is some kind of free-for-all display. He wisely nods. Puckers his lips. Sniffs. I know what he's going to say next and that it will make him very, very happy to say it.

"You are aware, of course, that you'll have to finish high school first. With good grades. Just when were you planning to get those?"

I feel a little nauseated. A little hot. A bit enraged. "To *get* them, sir?" I say innocently.

He slams down his hand flat on the desktop. I must jump about ten feet.

"Don't be smart with me! I've given you hours of my time. I've tried to reach you. I've been lenient with you. I've done everything I could to be the best possible friend I can. And I *am* your friend, Donald. But today just takes the cake. What are we going to do about it?"

"We?"

"Don't you know I could have you arrested right now? For trafficking? Don't you know that?"

"I wasn't selling drugs. And there's no such thing as brown cigarette papers. Name one time you have *ever* seen a brown cigarette paper, sir."

"Well. She was obviously wrong about the colour," he says, like he's thinking for the first time since I walked in here that he might be losing ground.

"She didn't see brown cigarette papers today," I say in a soft, respectful tone. "What she saw was a brown root beer can being cut up and rolled."

I sit back and wait to see what he'll do next. His face shows a real struggle. He's madly trying to stuff back whoever it is behind the vice-principal mask he dons every morning as he's getting that fat knot into his silk tie.

"A root beer can?"

"Would I make up such a thing?"

"Possibly. This may sound like a dumb question, Donald, but why would you be cutting up a root beer can?"

I take a deep breath. Might as well tell the truth. Who knows? He just might believe it.

"I was making an electric guitar, sir."

"Go on." He's got this steady bead on me, like if I blow this one I'm a dead man.

"A very small electric guitar. Not a real one, you understand, but something that looked like one. For a dead squirrel, sir. I made it so it would look as if he was really playing it. Sort of caught forever in the moment, if you know what I mean—kind of like a statue."

Flint crinkles up his forehead and allows this to register. He takes his pencil and sort of dances it between his hands. He then plops it into a stained white mug along with the other yellow pencils and cheap blue pens.

"Where is this squirrel?"

"He's lying on his back, sir, out in the school yard. I can show you if you like."

"And the guitar?"

"It's here in my pocket. I didn't have time to set him up yet, so to speak." The cold aluminum warms quickly in my fingers. "I actually didn't know if I felt like just leaving it out there, either. The guitar, I mean." I hold it out to Flint.

He takes it and studies it for a minute. Then he sort of sags over his desk.

"This actually resembles a guitar," he says, looking up at me with wonder on his face.

"Yes. I know it does," I say, suddenly very happy. It's only at this exact moment that I realize that it does. And that it's actually beautiful to look at. I start to laugh. My eyes smart.

"No. I mean truly it does," he says, pointing to the delicate strings. "How did you do those?"

"I cut the can up really fine there. I mean at that point of making it."

"You must have a *very* steady hand. This stuff looks almost *shaved.*"

"Well, I did sort of shave it. It was a kind of experimental shear-and-shave sort of thing."

"Does it actually fit the squirrel?"

"Yes, it does. We tried it out. It looks very lifelike."

"Believe me," he says, still looking at the guitar, "I know more than you think about what you're going through. You have an original turn of mind, Donald. If you could only find a way of using that to your benefit, instead of always using it like a suit of armour, then you'd have a sweet life."

"A sweet life?"

"Yes."

I wait for him to elaborate on this. He doesn't. He hands back my guitar. He plays with a pile of papers on his desk. "I pulled you out of your last class," he says, finally. "You might as well go on home now."

"Really? Thanks."

Flint's biggest problem is that he still likes kids, but we've finally worn him out.

I pause at the door, and on a kind of whim I say, "You really should be looking into another line of work, Mr. Eastwood.

Something that makes you feel happier."

"That would be terrific, Don," he says tiredly. "If I could only find the energy."

"You'll figure something out," I say.

I close the door as soft as a feather, so as not to jar his nerves any further.

I start down the hall. This is a small private school. I've been coming here ever since three-quarters of the way through first grade. The elementary school and the junior and senior high schools are separated by double glass doors. I don't often have a reason any more to be in the elementary part. But as I slide between the doors, I'm glad I came. I've entered another world—it's a trip back. Coloured construction paper taped to the walls, framed decorated poems entitled "What is Spring?" Some little kid has pasted cotton balls onto brown crayoned lines to show that SPRING IS PUSSY WILLOWS!

I'm thinking about my second-grade teacher, Miss Huska. She had black hair and green eyes and I fell in love with her on the first day back to school after Christmas vacation. My dad had left on New Year's—packed up as much as he could get into his big brown suitcase and left for good, and even though I didn't know exactly what was going on, like that I wouldn't see him from then on except sometimes in the summer, I felt sad and sick. At recess, when everyone else went outside, Miss Huska let me stay with her, indoors. That was when I decided to invite her to have lunch with me.

In the smaller grades, the teachers would sit down and have lunch with a student if they asked. First you had to write out a formal invitation (to improve your writing skills), and then they would write back. When I handed her my invitation with a picture of a lady and a boy eating lunch in their bathing suits (beside a big sand castle), she laughed and said, "Thank you, Don. This is for *me*?"

She always said, "This is for *me*?" like you'd just handed her a million bucks.

After the bell rang, we all sat in our desks for art class. Miss Huska smiled when she gave me her reply, which read, "Dear Don:

Yes, I will have lunch with you. Thank you for your gorgeous picture! And thank you for inviting me. Yours truly, Miss Huska."

That morning, in art class, I repeated in my mind the word *gorgeous*, like a prayer, as I made her three lime green tissue-paper roses. She put them in her pencil can, where they stayed for months and gradually got faded by sunlight until we were let out for the summer.

Outside the second-grade room, which used to be Miss Huska's class, a boy is sitting in the hall, on a sunny spot, his legs sprawled. He's flicking his chewed-up pencil against his knee. The door is closed, but I can still hear the voice of his teacher on the other side, raving on about arithmetic.

I shove my hand into my jacket pocket. I feel the feather-light strings of the guitar. The kid looks really bored, waiting by the door until his punishment is over. I push against the toe of his shoe to get his attention. He's skinny, with a grown-out brush cut. I hand over to him my work of art.

He looks at it, turns it upright, raises his eyebrows like a TV cartoon. He smiles. He has the kind of teeth that'll need braces in a couple of years.

I'm beginning to wonder if he appreciates what I've just handed him. I remember reading somewhere that art doesn't become art until it goes out into the world.

"It's yours," I say.

Even as I say it, part of me wants to take it back. It looks better and better in his hands. I can't believe I've created something so . . . gorgeous. That I actually did that. Finally I say, testy as hell, "Do you want it, or don't you?"

The kid pulls it to his chest, and my heart sinks. Then he gives me the craziest wink and starts madly fingering that tiniest guitar in the world like he's some big-time rocker.

He gets so involved that he doesn't even notice me leave, my boots clacking down the hall.

Outside, the sun is bright and the air is cold. On my way through the school grounds, I pass the squirrel, on his back, forever playing the invisible guitar. I'm grateful to him. Maybe I should make more stuff out of rejected junk material—a sort of personal statement on overlooked beauty.

I lean over, touch my right hand to my forehead, and salute him. After that, I turn and head home into the strong spring wind.

ACTIVITIES

DIRECTLY STATED IDEAS AND INFORMATION

1. What did the students find outside the school during lunch hour?

2. What did the narrator, Donald Petrie, make with the root beer can?

INDIRECTLY STATED IDEAS AND INFORMATION

3. Explain why Donald remembers his second-grade teacher and their lunch together so clearly.

4. Why did Donald give the guitar to the boy in the hall?

MAKING CONNECTIONS

5. Think of someone who has encouraged or supported you at some time in your life. What difference did that person make to the way you felt about yourself? Write a brief reflection.

WRITING EXTENSION

Pretend you are the vice-principal, Fletcher P. Eastwood. Write an incident report that summarizes the conversation you had with Donald and your conclusions about the incident. (Did Mr. Eastwood end up believing Donald?)

READING STRATEGY

Try the **Insert Note Taking** strategy. Write "+" on some sticky notes, and "?" on some other sticky notes. As you are reading, put the "+" notes beside new information you understand or find interesting and the "?" notes beside information you don't understand. At the end of the reading, copy this information into a two-column chart in your notebook.

Share the information on your chart with a partner or small group. Help one another to clear up the items in your "?" columns. Any items still remaining can be discussed as a class.

VOCABULARY PREVIEW

- epidemic
- idealized
- inadequate
- perceived
- desirable
- contemplate
- anorexic

The Search for the Perfect Body

❖ by Mary Walters Riskin

How do the media, particularly television, movies, and magazines, affect our view of the perfect body image?

Too tall! Too short! Too fat! Too thin! Too clumsy! Too weak!

Who do we say these negative things about? Not our friends. Not people we respect. Sometimes, maybe, we think or say them about people we don't like. But mostly they're said about ourselves. No matter how good you feel about your abilities and accomplishments, it's pretty difficult to be confident if you don't feel good about the way you look.

I hate the way I look.—Darlene, 15, a typical teenager

The present epidemic of self-dislike is related to the whole idea of "body image." Body image is really two images. One stares back at us when we look in the mirror: that's our Actual Body Image. The other is a mental picture of what we think we ought to look like: our Idealized Body Image.

Sometimes the Idealized Body Image is so firmly planted in our minds that it affects our judgement of the actual image in the mirror. We don't see our legs the way they really are—instead we see them compared to "how they ought to look." Instead of saying, "Those are my legs, not bad!" we say, "Those are my legs and they're too fat!" or "That's my nose and it's too big."

Walking away from the mirror, we feel inadequate and miserable. Unhappy with our perceived appearance, we can't relax or feel secure with other people. If you tell yourself over and over, "I'm ugly," you start to believe it and act like it's true. Self-confidence goes right out the window.

> I learned the truth at seventeen /
> that love was meant for beauty queens /
> and high-school girls with clear-skinned smiles...
> —Janis Ian, "At Seventeen"

Deep down, we know that there are things much more important than looks. When other people ask us what's important, we say, "Being kind," "Being friendly," or "Being loyal." But when we look in the mirror, we say to ourselves, "What's important is the way I look, and I don't look good enough."

Like our ideas about what's right or what's wrong, or about what's in or out, our ideas about ideal body image come from a number of places . . . starting with our parents and our friends. Even when we're very young, we see adults going on diets, working out, and worrying about the desserts they want to eat. People often apologize before eating, as if they were about to do something immoral. Have you ever made an excuse like, "I didn't eat all day," or "My blood sugar is low" before pigging out?

Kids who are overweight get teased and learn from the experience that bodies are supposed to be thin and muscular, and that there is one perfect body that everyone, especially us, must have.

The image of what that perfect body looks like hits us over and over in the media, particularly in television, movies, and magazines. TV programs and advertisements tell us that women should be thin and tall, with a small waist, slender thighs, and no hips; while height, large biceps, and strong thighs and quads are desirable in men.

Styles change over the years and this affects what people imagine the ideal body to look like. In the forties and fifties, the pudgy (by today's standards) Marilyn Monroe look was the style. In the early sixties, everyone wanted to be blond and tanned; the "Beach Boys" look was in. Today, blondes are unhappy because people make jokes about them, and tans are associated with over-age movie stars and with over-exposure to the sun, so the look has changed again.

One glance around the school or the shopping mall makes it clear that in the real world people come in every shape, size, age, and colour. But after looking at models and actors all day long, the fact that we don't look the way they do makes us feel inadequate.

When I was 18-years-old, and did look perfect, I was so insecure that I would face the wall in elevators because I knew the lighting was bad.
    —Cybill Shepherd, actor

We're "too fat" compared to whom? "Too short" compared to whom? Sometimes the perfect body we're looking for doesn't even belong to the person we think it does.

But we continue to diet, exercise, and contemplate the cost of plastic surgery, trying to turn ourselves into people we can't be. Some people make themselves exhausted and even sick with starvation diets to lose weight or with drugs to improve their strength, only to discover that no matter what they do, they're still not happy with the way they look.

She ain't pretty; she just looks that way.—The Northern Pikes

With so many unhappy people lacking self-esteem and a positive self-image, sales of hair-dyes, make-up, exercise equipment, and diet plans are booming. People want to buy things because they think they'll make them perfect. And perfect is happy. Well, at least the advertisers are happy!

There's some evidence that things are changing. Magazines such as *Sports Illustrated* are actually telling their models to gain a few pounds. Suddenly, the anorexic look is out. Not every character on television has to be perfect anymore, and some TV shows . . . have made a genuine effort to portray people the way they really are. But there's still a lot of room for improvement.

If I spent my life worrying about what I didn't like about myself, I'd never have fun.—Susan, 15

While we're waiting for the media to change, we can change ourselves. Not our bodies, but our attitudes. We can stop playing the Ideal Body Image game in our heads. We can accept that the way we are right now is okay. We look like us, and each one of us is different. When we start to focus on ourselves as individuals, we begin to develop the self-confidence behind the most attractive look of all.

> I look like this because I want to. I like looking like this.
> —Sinead O'Connor

ACTIVITIES

DIRECTLY STATED IDEAS AND INFORMATION

1. According to the author, what is the difference between an Idealized Body Image and an Actual Body Image?

2. Explain in your own words why people get ideas of what's right and what's wrong about ideal body image.

INDIRECTLY STATED IDEAS AND INFORMATION

3. The author includes quotations from other people throughout this selection. Why has she included quotations from both celebrities and ordinary teenagers?

4. Explain why you think "The Search for the Perfect Body" is (or is not) a good title for this reading selection.

MAKING CONNECTIONS

5. The author suggests that "there's some evidence that things are changing." Look for evidence in media or other sources to back up or refute this claim.

WRITING EXTENSION

Summarize this article in 150 words or less. Make sure you include the author's main idea and the details that she uses to support this idea.

READING STRATEGY

As you read this poem, think about who Christine is, and who is talking to her.

VOCABULARY PREVIEW

◆ punishing

◆ ideal

◆ against

To Christine

❖ by Susan Forde

I wish I could tell you
That you're not too fat
That you're fine the way that you are
That you're pretty enough
And you don't have to wear punishing heels
I wish I could make you believe
That you don't have to starve yourself
Or add to your chest
To fit this year's fashions.
And I wish I could tell you,
To love yourself as much as you love him.
You don't have to make yourself
Into his ideal
The real you is worth so much more.
But I am only one voice,
Against so many
The magazines with diets and makeovers
That you read
The fairy tale your mother read you,
Where the mermaid gave her voice
To be what the prince wanted.
Oh, I wish I could make you listen
But I'm only one voice
Drowned out by so many.

ACTIVITIES

DIRECTLY STATED IDEAS AND INFORMATION

1. What did the mermaid give to be what the prince wanted?

2. What is one way Christine changes her appearance to make herself "pretty enough"?

INDIRECTLY STATED IDEAS AND INFORMATION

3. Explain whether you think Christine will believe the message in the poem that she is fine the way she is. Give evidence from the poem to back up your answer. What are the "so many" voices that are drowning out the author's voice?

4. The author writes, "To love yourself as much as you love him." Who is the "him" she is referring to?

MAKING CONNECTIONS

5. This poem focuses on the social pressure felt by teenage girls to look and act a certain way. What are the social pressures on teenage boys? In small groups, discuss what ideals are held up to young men. Do you think there is more pressure on males or females in our society?

WRITING EXTENSION

In three well-developed paragraphs, explain whether or not you think the media affect the way young women see themselves. Use specific examples from television, magazines, or other media to back up your point of view.

READING STRATEGY
Examine the ad close up and from a distance. How do the different views change the effect of the poster?

Eating Disorders Poster

London, Paris, NewYork or Somalia?

Because of the tremendous pressure to be thin, many female models starve themselves. To the point where they end up anorexic, bulimic or, in very extreme cases, dead. Next time you go on a diet, ask yourself, who are you modelling yourself after? The National Eating Disorder Information Centre. It's not our bodies that need changing. It's our attitudes. College Wing 1-211, 200 Elizabeth St. Toronto Ontario M5G 2C4

ACTIVITIES

DIRECTLY STATED IDEAS AND INFORMATION

1. Explain the choice of locations mentioned in the text box.

2. Summarize in your own words the text of this poster.

INDIRECTLY STATED IDEAS AND INFORMATION

3. What emotion is the woman in the poster expressing?

4. How does the arrangement of text and visual contribute to the message?

MAKING CONNECTIONS

5. When you look at the poster, what has the most impact at first—the visual or the words? How has the creator used light and dark to make the visual more effective?

WRITING EXTENSION

"Who are you modelling yourself after?" Use this question from the poster as the basis for a brief written reflection on public figures, celebrities, or media images that influence your own self-image. Who, if anyone, do you compare yourself to?

Aim for success, not perfection. Never give up your right to be wrong, because then you will lose the ability to learn new things and move forward with your life.

— *David M. Burns*
Doctor

READING STRATEGY

Before you read the words on this advertisement, look at the picture. Write a sentence **predicting** what the advertisement will be about. After you read the text, go back and re-read your prediction. How close were you?

VOCABULARY PREVIEW

◆ unfortunate
◆ insignificant
◆ impact
◆ essential
◆ standards

Special K Ad

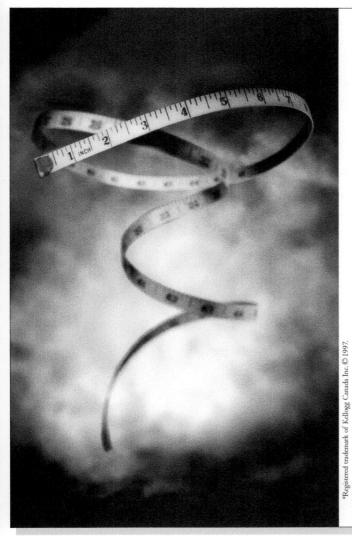

DON'T LET IT MEASURE YOUR SELF-ESTEEM.

It's unfortunate that something as insignificant as a tape measure can have such an impact on how we feel about ourselves. Don't let it. It can't measure who you are. Exercise. Refuse to skip meals. Start with a balanced breakfast every morning and go from there. Kellogg's Special K* cereal is fat free and a source of nine essential nutrients so it's a light, sensible way to start your day. After all, looking your best is about being strong and healthy. And the standards you measure yourself by should be your own.

*Registered trademark of Kellogg Canada Inc. © 1997.

Kellogg's
Special K
www.specialk.ca

Look good on your own terms.

ACTIVITIES

DIRECTLY STATED IDEAS AND INFORMATION

1. List three things that this advertisement says you should do to be strong and healthy.

2. In your own words, explain the main message of the ad.

INDIRECTLY STATED IDEAS AND INFORMATION

3. The word "measure" is used four times in this piece. Explain the significance of this word (hint: look at the picture).

4. What audience do you think this ad is aimed at? Give reasons for your answer.

MAKING CONNECTIONS

5. Only one sentence in the ad mentions the product being sold. Why do you think the company decided to present their product in this way?

WRITING EXTENSION

Based on the information in this ad and your own knowledge, write an information paragraph called "Ways to Live a Healthier Lifestyle." Address your advice to people your own age.

READING STRATEGY

Before you read this selection, think about your attitude toward ghosts. Is it possible that they exist? Or are they just fragments of people's imaginations? As you read, consider how your opinion affects your reaction to the story.

VOCABULARY PREVIEW

- ◆ encouraged
- ◆ mocking
- ◆ scrambled
- ◆ evidence
- ◆ encounter
- ◆ credibility

Murder Revealed

❖ by Pat Hancock

Russian stonemason Ivan Reznikoff was pleased with his new job in Canada. Like several other foreign stonemasons, he had been encouraged to come to Toronto where his skills were in great demand. In 1885 he was working on the new University College building at the University of Toronto. The money was good, his savings were growing, and he was in love. In fact, his girlfriend, Susie, had just accepted his marriage proposal.

One day, Reznikoff was carving the finishing touches on a large stone head, or gargoyle, that would peer down on passersby when it was done. Several other stonemasons worked alongside him on the detailed carvings that would decorate the upper levels of the building's exterior. During a break, one of the men leaned over and asked Ivan if he recognized the gargoyle that another stonemason, a Greek named Paul Diabolos, was chiselling nearby.

At first glance Ivan didn't notice anything familiar about the head. The figures' mouths usually served as waterspouts draining rain off the roof, and their faces were usually distorted to look rather menacing. But when the man who had spoken to him pointed out that Diabolos was making the gargoyle look like Ivan, the young Russian saw what he meant. There was definitely a resemblance between himself and the Greek's wild-eyed stone creation. But why would Diabolos do this? Ivan wondered aloud. His co-worker replied the Greek was mocking him, because he

hadn't realized that his fiancée, Susie, was seeing Diabolos despite her engagement to Reznikoff.

Though Reznikoff was filled with rage, he said nothing. Instead, he spent the rest of the day gouging out new features on his gargoyle to transform it into a hideous sculpture of Diabolos. And that night, armed with an axe, Ivan hid in the bushes near the arched walkway at the university where his informant had said the couple usually met. Right after dark he saw them—Susie and Diabolos—walking hand in hand along the path to the arch. He watched in silence as they sat on a bench and talked, heads close together as if sharing secrets. But when they embraced and kissed passionately, he lost control.

Reznikoff burst from the bushes and raced towards them, swinging the axe. Diabolos jumped up and ran for his life. He dashed into University College and closed the heavy oak door just in time to hear the axe hit it with a thud. He scrambled up a temporary set of wooden stairs in the unfinished stone tower and hid in an alcove. Reznikoff followed, but when he climbed out on the top platform, Diabolos lunged at him with a knife. After stabbing the Russian, he pushed Reznikoff over the edge of the platform and into the 25-metre-deep well where the tower's stone steps were to go.

Diabolos might have been able to make a good case for self-defence, but there's no record of that happening. There's also no evidence that anyone even bothered to report the unfortunate Reznikoff's sudden disappearance. But in the early 1860s, both professors and students started talking about a tall, handsome stranger they'd seen moving about the campus late at night. A few even said that he carried an axe. Whenever anyone tried to speak with him, he mysteriously disappeared.

One night a student named Allen Aylesworth was returning to his dormitory when he met a young man he didn't recognize. Assuming the fellow was a new arrival on campus, Aylesworth started up a friendly conversation with him. After a few minutes, he invited the stranger back to his room for a drink. After downing a couple of shots of whisky, the stranger stunned Aylesworth by telling him something unbelievable. He said that his name was Ivan Reznikoff and that he was a ghost. He proceeded to talk about his beloved Susie, her betrayal of him with Diabolos and his horrible death at the hands of the Greek. Then he said goodnight and left.

When Aylesworth awoke the next morning, he remembered his encounter with Reznikoff, but figured it must have been a bad dream. Ghosts—if they existed—didn't just come up and introduce themselves and join you for a drink. Then Aylesworth looked across the room. There on the table were two glasses and an empty liquor bottle.

Word of Aylesworth's eerie experience spread quickly around the university. From then on, whenever people spotted the ghostly apparition of a tall, heavy-set man around University College, they said it must be Reznikoff. In 1890 that explanation started sounding even more believable when the skeletal remains of a large unidentified male were dug up during construction near the base of the college tower. And when old records turned up showing that two stonemasons named Reznikoff and Diabolos had indeed worked at the college, more people became convinced that Aylesworth's tale must have been true. Anyone who still doubted Aylesworth's credibility as a witness may have had second thoughts when he became a member of Parliament and was later knighted.

Then there's the gouge in the old oak door, said to be made by Reznikoff's axe. It's still there for all to see. And off to one side, glaring down from above, are two expertly carved stone gargoyles.

ACTIVITIES

DIRECTLY STATED IDEAS AND INFORMATION

1. Why was Reznikoff so angry when he saw Susie and Diabolos "kissing passionately"? Why did Reznikoff chase after Diabolos?

2. Look at the photograph. What does it show?

INDIRECTLY STATED IDEAS AND INFORMATION

3. What reason would Reznikoff's co-worker have for telling him about Susie and Diabolos?

4. What is one piece of evidence that supports the fact that Reznikoff became a ghost?

MAKING CONNECTIONS

5. Explain whether you believe that Reznikoff was haunting the university. Back up your answer with information from the text or your own experience.

WRITING EXTENSION

Pretend that you are a newspaper reporter in 1858. Write a news article about Reznikoff's disappearance. Include important facts about what happened (who, what, when, where, why, how) near the beginning of the article. Think of a good headline for your report.

READING STRATEGY

Make a **story map** like the one below in your notebook. After reading the story, complete each box using point-form notes. Did knowing you would fill in the story map change the way you read and understood the story?

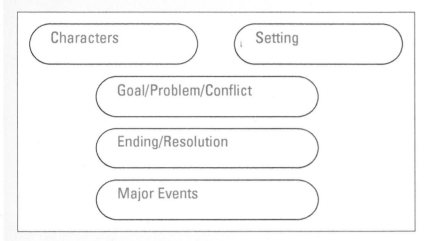

- Characters
- Setting
- Goal/Problem/Conflict
- Ending/Resolution
- Major Events

VOCABULARY PREVIEW

- malice
- mute
- ascribe
- antagonism
- insurmountable
- descent

Barney
A Fictional Diary

❖ by Will Stanton

August 30th. We are alone on the island now, Barney and I. It was something of a jolt to have to sack Tayloe after all these years, but I had no alternative. The petty vandalisms I could have forgiven, but when he tried to poison Barney out of simple malice, he was standing in the way of scientific progress. That I cannot condone. I can only believe the attempt was made under the influence of alcohol, it was so clumsy. The poison container was overturned and a trail of powder led to Barney's dish. Tayloe's defense was of the flimsiest. He denied it. Who else then?

September 2nd. I am taking a calmer view of the Tayloe affair. The monastic life here must have become too much for him. That, and the abandonment of his precious guinea pigs. He insisted to the last that they were better suited than Barney to my experiments. They were more his speed, I'm afraid. He was an earnest and willing worker, but something of a clod, poor fellow. At last I have complete freedom to carry on my work without the mute reproaches of Tayloe. I can only ascribe his violent antagonism toward Barney to jealousy. And now that he has gone, how much happier Barney appears to be! I have given him complete run of the place, and what sport it is to observe how his newly awakened intellectual curiosity carries him about. After only two weeks of glutamic acid treatments, he has become interested in my library, dragging the books from the shelves, and going over them page by page. I am certain he knows there is some knowledge to be gained from them had he but the key.

September 8th. For the past two days I have had to keep Barney confined and how he hates it. I am afraid that when my experiments are completed I shall have to do away with Barney. Ridiculous as it may sound there is still the possibility that he might be able to communicate his intelligence to others of his kind. However small the chance may be, the risk is too great to ignore. Fortunately there is, in the basement, a vault built with the idea of keeping vermin out and it will serve equally well to keep Barney in.

September 9th. Apparently I have spoken too soon. This morning I let him out to frisk around a bit before commencing a new series of tests. After a quick survey of the room he returned to his cage, sprang up on the door handle, removed the key with his teeth, and before I could stop him, he was out the window. By the time I reached the yard I spied him on the coping of the well, and I arrived on the spot only in time to hear the key splash into the water below. I own I am somewhat embarrassed. It is the only key. The door is locked. Some valuable papers are in separate compartments inside the vault. Fortunately, although the well is over forty feet deep, there are only a few feet of water in the bottom, so the retrieving of the key does not present an insurmountable obstacle. But I must admit Barney has won the first round.

September 10th. I have had a rather shaking experience, and once more in a minor clash with Barney I have come off second best. In this instance I will admit he played the hero's role and may even have saved my life. In order to facilitate my descent into the well I knotted a length of three-quarter-inch rope at one-foot intervals to make a rude ladder. I reached the bottom easily enough, but after only a few minutes of groping for the key, my flashlight gave out and I returned to the surface. A few feet from the top I heard excited squeaks from Barney, and upon obtaining ground level I observed that the rope was almost completely severed. Apparently it had chafed against the edge of the masonry and the little fellow perceiving my plight had been doing his utmost to warn me. I have now replaced that section of rope and arranged some old sacking beneath it to prevent a recurrence of the accident. I have replenished the batteries in my flashlight and am now prepared for the final descent. These few moments I have taken off to give myself a breathing spell and to bring my journal up to date. Perhaps I should fix myself a sandwich as I may be down there longer than seems likely at the moment.

September 11th. Poor Barney is dead an soon I shell be the same. He was a wonderful ratt and life without him is knot worth livving. If anybody reeds this please do not disturb anything on the island but leeve it like it is a shryn to Barney, espechilly the old well. Do not look for my body as I will caste myself into the see. You mite bring a couple of young ratts an leeve them as a living memorial to Barney. Females no males. I sprayned my wrist is why this is written so bad. This is my last will. Do what I say an don't come back or disturb anything after you bring the young ratts like I said. Just females.

Goodby

ACTIVITIES

DIRECTLY STATED IDEAS AND INFORMATION

1. What did the author give to Barney that made him smarter?

2. What type of animal did Tayloe want to use in the experiments?

INDIRECTLY STATED IDEAS AND INFORMATION

3. Why did Tayloe deny trying to poison Barney?

4. How did the rope get severed while the scientist was climbing into the well?

5. Explain why the author of the September 11th entry wants female rats shipped to the island.

MAKING CONNECTIONS

6. Explain whether you think the scientists treated Barney fairly.

WRITING EXTENSION

You are a journalist who goes to the island to interview the scientists. Instead, you find only the journal. Write a newspaper account of what happened, titled "Science Gone Wrong!" Begin with a paragraph that summarizes the main events (your story map may be helpful here). Then add background information and end with a concluding statement. Include at least one quotation.

Reflecting on Your Learning

This section will give you a chance to think back over the past unit, reflect upon what you have learned, and apply it to your future learning.

READING SKILLS

1. Which of the reading selections in this unit did you like the best? Why? Which one did you like least? Why?

2. Skim the selections you read in this unit to remind yourself what they were about. Then find a way to categorize them (by form, topic, features, purpose, or in another way). Copy the chart below into your notebook and fill it in.

	Category One	Category Two	Category Three	Category Four
Category Description				
Selections				

Using the information from this chart, make a bar graph of the selections you read in this unit.

WRITING /COMMUNICATION SKILLS

3. After completing this unit, what is one thing you have learned to do when writing a summary, informative piece, news story, or opinion piece that you didn't do before?

4. How could your knowledge of how to write one of these forms help you to become a better reader of that form?

LEARNING SKILLS

5. Give specific examples of attitudes or behaviours you can adopt that will help you to succeed in this course.

LOOKING AHEAD

6. Based on all of the information above, set two learning goals for yourself for the next few weeks.

Belonging to Communities

We all belong to communities. Sometimes, these are actual places on a map—a village, town, or big-city neighbourhood. Other times, communities are made up of people with similar backgrounds or interests—anything from driving to skateboarding to talking online. In this unit, you'll read about all these kinds of communities, and look at some of the ways that group members communicate with one another.

READING STRATEGY

*Use the **Insert Note Taking** strategy for this selection. See page 60 for instructions. You might consider adding other symbols to your sticky notes to record your reaction to this piece. Use the symbols below, or make up your own. When you have finished, share your marks with another student or with the class.*

+ *something I didn't know*
! *wow!*
? *I don't understand*
* *important*
x *I disagree*

VOCABULARY PREVIEW

- self-segregation
- Hispanic
- intriguing
- lexicon
- christened
- dialect
- radiated
- prejudice
- brigade
- complicit
- revile
- integration

Small Town Ways

❖ by June Chua

Self-segregation. The word caught my ear during a CBC Radio special about America. The reporter was doing a feature about middle- or upper-class black and Hispanic people choosing to live in neighbourhoods where people of their own race or culture lived.

It's always intriguing when new words enter the lexicon because behind every new word is an old idea. Self-segregation isn't limited to our neighbours to the south. It has occurred in Canada ever since immigrants started populating this land.

When you're a stranger in a strange land, a city seems so much more attractive: neighbourhoods where people speak your language and stores where you can buy goods from the homeland. It's a way of hiding and

keeping the rest of the population at bay. Them and us.

Not to diss cities—I've lived in seven of them around the world—but my heart lies in a town called Oyen, huddled against the Alberta/Saskatchewan border.

When my family arrived from Malaysia in 1976, my parents wanted to settle in Vancouver because we had friends there. But my dad, a civil engineer with a degree from St. Mary's in Halifax, couldn't find a job.

When a friend commented that the streets of Alberta were paved with gold, Dad packed us into a second-hand forest green station wagon and drove us—Mom, me and my two sisters—east to Calgary. We christened the station wagon the Green Bomb.

Alberta was in the midst of the oil boom. A small engineering firm decided to take Dad on, with one proviso—would he mind moving to a small town called Oyen for six months? We headed off again in the Green Bomb into the blue infinity of the Alberta sky.

Oyen had only 5000 people. The only other Asian family in town owned the Chinese restaurant. The food was weird. Chicken balls? They didn't speak our dialect. We were Chinese from Malaysia, they weren't. They were as foreign to us as the Canadians.

We discovered our first home in Canada was a three-bedroom trailer in a trailer park! Incredible, a house on wheels. We loved it.

The next day, a knock on the door. "Hi! I'm Ruby, Harvey's wife? He's working with your husband. Welcome to Oyen. Here's some pie I baked."

Ruby had one glass eye and warmth that radiated beyond the blue sky. We were enchanted. She marched in with her three kids—two boys and a girl—all corresponding to our ages. Her daughter Trina became a close friend to all three of us girls.

Trina, Ruby, and Harvey helped us adjust. Ruby showed my mother where the Laundromat was and how to work it, and introduced us to other families. We ate at their place occasionally, having mashed potatoes and roast beef with gravy (. . . mmmmm!). This was real Canadian food.

We enrolled in school in September. Every morning we sang "God Save the Queen" and had our fingernails inspected by a student. We got little gold stars if our nails were clean.

We were probably the only minorities in that school but we were never called names. Not so, in the city.

Canadian comedian Sean Majumder has also recalled fondly growing up in rural Canada—as a member of the only Pakistani family in a rural town. Coincidentally, Majumder lived in a trailer and says his family didn't encounter the same prejudice some Pakistanis endured elsewhere in the country.

I think Majumder has said it before: the more you hide yourself from the community around you, the less they know you or understand you.

Perhaps the Majumders and my family were fortunate in one sense. We spoke English, or rather, the Queen's English. My mother would often be met with puzzlement and laughter if she referred to garbage as "rubbish," the back of the car as "the boot," or to an eraser as the "rubber."

In Oyen, we experienced our first Halloween—no other would measure up in the years after. An older girl in town offered to take us trick-or-treating. I can still feel the goose-pimply excitement of embarking on this candy brigade.

We spent Christmas with Ruby and her family. My dad got drunk, his face beet-red from the wine, and belted out songs with Harvey while Ruby played the piano. We laughed till we cried.

With the new year came the move to Calgary. A new home, a new neighbourhood, and a new school. For the first time, someone in the schoolyard made a rude comment about my ethnic background. I learned a new word. I felt like ripping off my skin and pointing out that I had the same insides as he did.

The experience of being in Canada lost its magic. No one offered to take us trick-or-treating and there was no Ruby bearing pie and friendliness.

While there is a lot of acceptance of foreigners in a city, there is still a lot of underlying mistrust. Them and us. With self-segregation, people become complicit in causing the racism that they claim to revile.

What my family gained from our Oyen experience was the real sense of who Canadians were and what they stood for: tolerance, kindness, and a sincere openness that ran counter to the harsh weather.

Unwittingly, my family experienced a gentle integration into the Canadian landscape. It was as complete as anyone who had been born here and it all happened in a town called Oyen.

ACTIVITIES

DIRECTLY STATED IDEAS AND INFORMATION

1. What reasons does the author give for the fact that many immigrants find cities more attractive than small towns?

2. Create a chart in which you contrast the speaker's memories of life in a small town with her memories of life in a city.

INDIRECTLY STATED IDEAS AND INFORMATION

3. According to the author, how do people "self-segregate" themselves in Canada?

4. What does the author mean when she refers to "them and us" in the third paragraph?

MAKING CONNECTIONS

5. What experience have you had of being "a stranger in a strange land"? What exactly does this phrase mean to you?

WRITING EXTENSION

Using the chart you created in question 2, write a summary of June Chua's experiences in the small town of Oyen and in the city of Calgary. Remember to include the most important ideas, and to write in your own words.

READING STRATEGY

Read the song lyrics. Then, if possible, listen to a recording of the song. How does hearing the music change your impression of the song?

VOCABULARY PREVIEW

◆ romantic

◆ hayseed

Small Town

❖ by John Cougar Mellencamp

Well, I was born in a small town
And I live in a small town
Prob'ly die in a small town
Oh, those small communities

All my friends are so small town
My parents live in the same small town
My job is so small town
Provides little opportunity

Educated in a small town
Taught the fear of Jesus in a small town
Used to daydream in that small town
Another boring romantic that's me

I've seen it all in a small town
Had myself a ball in a small town
Married an L.A. doll and brought her to this small town
Now she's small town just like me

No, I cannot forget where it is that I come from
I cannot forget the people who love me
Yeah, I can be myself here in this small town
And people let me be just what I want to be

Got nothing against a big town
Still hayseed enough to say
Look who's in the big town
But my bed is in a small town

Well, I was born in a small town
And I can breathe in a small town
Gonna die in this small town
And that's prob'ly where they'll bury me . . .

ACTIVITIES

DIRECTLY STATED IDEAS AND INFORMATION

1. Why does the speaker prefer the small town he grew up in?

2. What negative aspects of life in a small town does the song mention?

INDIRECTLY STATED IDEAS AND INFORMATION

3. Count the number of times "small town" is repeated throughout this song. What effect does this have?

4. Do you think that the speaker would leave the town he lives in, given the chance? Why?

MAKING CONNECTIONS

5. How would you describe life in your community? Describe both good and bad aspects of living there.

WRITING EXTENSION

Arrange some of the ideas from question 5 to create a poem or song about your community.

Go confidently in the direction of
your dreams. Live the life you have
imagined.

— *Henry David Thoreau (1817–1962)*
Writer

READING STRATEGY

Before reading this textbook excerpt, **skim** the title, headings, and visuals. Turn each heading into a question. Then read the section to find the answer.

VOCABULARY PREVIEW

- culturally diverse
- wares
- enticing
- persecution
- haven
- ethnic

Case Study: Kensington Market, Toronto

❖ by Colin M. Bain

One of the most famous culturally diverse areas in Canada is Toronto's Kensington Market. It takes up about five square city blocks in an area just west of the downtown, and right on the border of Chinatown. The streets of Kensington are narrow and lined with old red-brick houses. The many small shops along the streets display their wares on the sidewalks, enticing shoppers to enter. A variety of delicious smells fill the air— everything from salted fish to fresh baked bread to exotic spices.

History

The land that would later become known as Kensington Market was originally the home of the Ojibwa. They fished and traded beside the lakes and rivers of the region. Europeans began to arrive in the 1790s. Wealthy aristocrats were offered parcels of land to encourage them to build large homes in the area. But many chose to sell off smaller lots to less wealthy tradespeople who had recently emigrated from Britain and Ireland. This created an area with close-set houses and narrow streets.

After 1900, the first wave of immigrants were replaced by Jewish (and some Italian)

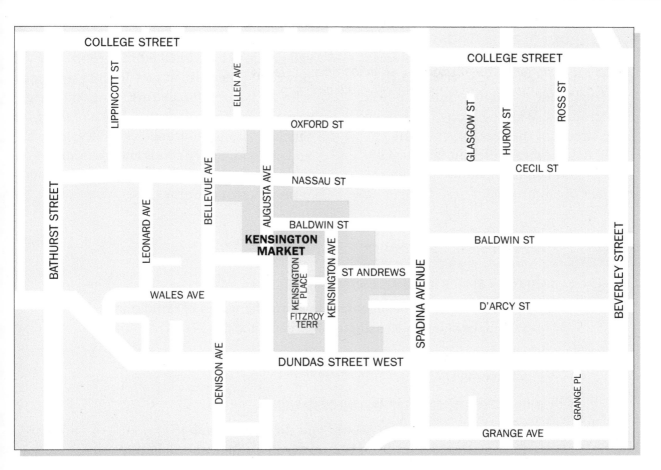

immigrants. Many of these newcomers were fleeing war, poverty, and persecution at home. They introduced the custom of selling wares from carts. Eventually, the carts were abandoned, and people's houses became storefronts. The area became known as the Jewish Market.

Although the area remained mostly Jewish until the 1950s, other immigrants also left their mark on Kensington. Along with Ukrainians, Hungarians, and Italians, large numbers of Portuguese moved in. This last group were the main residents of the area by the 1960s. They opened stores selling fish and other Portuguese foods.

Many painted their houses in bright colours, as is the custom in Portugal.

In the late 1960s and 1970s, Americans trying to escape being drafted for the war in Vietnam came to Kensington. Chinese people also moved in, as Toronto's Chinatown expanded westward.

From 1975 on, a huge wave of immigrants from over thirty cultural backgrounds, including South American, South Asian, African, and Caribbean, have found a haven in Kensington Market. These immigrants include people looking for better opportunities as well as some fleeing persecution.

Kensington Market Today

Today, Kensington Market is an ethnically diverse neighbourhood—that is, it has residents from an exciting mix of ethnic backgrounds. Walking along the narrow, busy streets of the market, you will likely hear several different languages spoken and run into people from any number of countries.

The market still has specialty stores that sell goods to individual ethnic groups. But nowadays, they also attract Toronto residents who are looking for an interesting shopping experience. You will find all kinds of things to buy here, from fruits and vegetables, to meat and seafood, to dry goods and clothing. At the many restaurants and cafés, you can try foods from different countries and cultures.

ACTIVITIES

DIRECTLY STATED IDEAS AND INFORMATION

1. Create a timeline or organizer to show the waves of immigrants who have come to Kensington Market since the 1700s.

2. Where is Kensington Market located in relation to Chinatown?

INDIRECTLY STATED IDEAS AND INFORMATION

3. Look at the map. How would you direct someone to Kensington Market from the corner of Grange and Beverley?

4. Name three things about Kensington Market that might attract people from outside the area to shop there.

MAKING CONNECTIONS

5. Kensington Market also attracts a lot of tourists. What do you think would attract tourists in your area? Describe one local tourist attraction, and explain what you think visitors might find interesting about it.

WRITING EXTENSION

Write a summary of the changes that have occurred in the Kensington Market neighbourhood over the years. Use your notes from question 1.

The United Way

UNITED
WE CARE!

Four-year-old Matthew has cerebral palsy. He and his parents Sonya and Jeff get tremendous support from Extend-A-Family, a United Way Member Agency.

United Way
SERVING KITCHENER-WATERLOO
And the Townships of Wellesley, Wilmot and Woolwich

UNITED WAY FOCUS

THROUGHOUT THE YEARS, during times of prosperity and hardship, United Way has been at the forefront of social change.

United Way continually assesses the community to ensure that funding meets the most urgent challenges.

- Giving young children a healthy start in life.

- Providing older children and youth with the support and guidance needed to make good choices.

- Welcoming newcomers and refugees by supporting their full participation in community life.

- Giving support to families to help them cope with a crisis or hard times.

- Improving the quality of life for seniors and people with disabilities.

UNITED WAY IS HERE FOR YOU

FOR 62 YEARS, our community has supported United Way. Today our commitment to building a better community is stronger than ever.

United Way is the largest non-government source of funding for social service programs in the community.

- United Way funds 80 programs at 45 community agencies, to provide the best results for people in Kitchener, Waterloo, and the townships of Wellesley, Wilmot, and Woolwich.

- The money we raise stays in the K-W area. In 2002, a record $5.1 MILLION was celebrated in the fundraising campaign. Thanks to your generosity more money was invested into our community.

- Trained community volunteers ensure that your gifts are distributed to programs and services that make a positive difference.

See how your

log on

BENEFITS OF GIVING

When you give to United Way, you are making a wise investment for a stronger and healthier community. Your gift makes a difference!

- **Donating** to United Way is a substantial investment in our community; each donation is directed to where it will do the most good.

- **Supporting** United Way demonstrates your willingness to participate in positive community changes and impact the lives of thousands of individuals and families this year.

- **Contributing** to United Way allows you to be part of the solution and help foster positive changes for the future.

HOW YOU CAN HELP

Healthy communities are essential to everyone's prosperity, safety, and comfort. Through generosity, this community can continue to flourish.

Workplace donation – If your company runs a workplace campaign, participate in the payroll deduction plan.

Give from home – You may contribute to the United Way campaign by mail or log onto our website at www.united-way-kw.org.

Become a Leadership donor – A pledge of $1,000 or more distinguishes you as a United Way Leader.

Valon and Jetmir, new immigrants from Kosovo, attend the Newcomer Youth Support Program at the YMCA of Kitchener-Waterloo.

a difference.

e at:

ACTIVITIES

DIRECTLY STATED IDEAS AND INFORMATION

1. Where is the most important information in the pamphlet located?

2. What sections is the information divided up into?

INDIRECTLY STATED IDEAS AND INFORMATION

3. How many times do you see the word "you" in the pamphlet? Why do you think this word is repeated so often?

4. Find at least three text features in this pamphlet, and describe what effect they have on the reader.

MAKING CONNECTIONS

5. What other types of organizations are faced with the task of motivating people, year after year, to get involved or donate money? Make a list, and then discuss which campaigns are most memorable.

WRITING EXTENSION

The United Way has asked you to create a new design for their pamphlet. How would you design it? How would you change this message to make it more specific to your community? Write a one-page description of the changes you would make, along with your reasons for making them.

READING STRATEGY

Use the **VOC** strategy to learn and remember some of the new vocabulary from this selection. Choose four terms from the Vocabulary Preview list that you are not sure of. Before you read, write down what you think each one means. Then read the selection and find the sentence in which each term appears. Revise your definition based on how it is used in this sentence.

When you have finished reading, check a dictionary, or consult an expert to find the actual meaning of the term. Write a sentence to show this meaning. Then find a way to remember the meaning of the word.

VOCABULARY PREVIEW

- Pearl Harbour
- Japanese Zeros
- barricaded
- Thai
- lemongrass
- notoriously
- saunter
- nomadic
- conversion
- spawned
- peruse
- urbane

The Urban Indian

❖ by Drew Hayden Taylor

I was visiting my mother on the Reserve when it hit me.

I had been out for a country walk in the quiet evening air when I noticed something I hadn't seen since last year: a single, tiny mosquito. And as is the mosquito mentality, within an incredibly short period of time, they were everywhere. And I do mean everywhere! Feeling like I was Pearl Harbour and the mosquitoes were Japanese Zeros, I fled.

As I scooted in through the door [of my mother's house], barricaded behind the window screening, I noticed my mother and aunts laughing quietly. Their one statement revealed a sad but true reality:

"You've been in the city too long."

I have spent years denying it, ignoring the evidence, but I just can't do it anymore. I have reached a point of personal awareness in my life where I must face certain unavoidable realities, no matter how painful. After 16 years of living in Canada's largest city I have finally admitted to myself the painful truth: I . . . am . . . an . . .urban Indian.

Not that I have anything against urban Indians. Some of my best friends are urban Indians. In fact, most of my friends are urban Indians. I just never thought I would ever be one. In just two more years I'll have spent exactly half my life in Toronto, drinking café au laits, eating in Thai restaurants (it's hard to find good lemongrass soup on the reserve), riding the subways (also notoriously difficult to locate on a reserve), and having pizza delivered to my door. I've grown soft.

A long time ago I heard an elder wisely say to a group of young people, "We must go from being hunters in the forest to being hunters in the city." I now hunt for a good dry-cleaners.

By trade I am a writer (though some might argue). I write plays, scripts, and short stories—all, oddly enough, taking place on an Indian reserve. In the past I used this simple fact to tell myself that although my body lived in an apartment near Bathurst and St. Clair, my spirit was somehow fishing in an unspoiled, unpolluted lake, nestled in the bosom of Mother Earth, somewhere up near Peterborough, Ontario.

Work and education were the reasons I originally came to Toronto those many years and fewer pounds ago. I sought to explore the world outside the reserve boundaries and taste what the world had to offer. As with all things in life, there is a give and take involved in exploration. Instead of the easy "I'll-get-there-when-I-get-there" saunter so many of my "rez" brothers and sisters have, I now have my own "I have to get there in the next five minutes or life as I know it will end" hustle.

I've traded roving the back roads in pick-up trucks for weaving in and out of traffic on my bicycle. Where once I camped on deserted islands, I now get a thrill out of ordering room service in a hotel.

Somehow, it loses something in translation.

Unfortunately, there are many people who live on these reserves who feel you aren't a proper Native person unless you are born, live and die on that little piece of land put aside by the government to contain Indians. How quickly they forget most aboriginal nations were nomadic in nature. When I tell these people "take a hike," I mean it in the most aboriginal of contexts.

I don't have to explain to my critics that I've spent 18 years growing up in that rural community. It shaped who I am and what I am, and if psychologists are correct, barring any serious religious conversion, I should remain roughly the same. The reserve is still deep within me. Given a few seconds of preparation, I can still remember the lyrics to most of Charley Pride's greatest hits. I can remember who the original six hockey teams were. And I know that contrary to popular belief, fried foods are actually good for you.

There is always the opinion, of course, that someday, if the Gods permit, I could return to the community that spawned me. As my mother says, I know home will always be there. So will the mosquitoes and the gossip and relatives who still treat you like you were twelve years old—and those who walk in my moccasins know the rest.

Until then, if there is a then, I shall be content to acknowledge my current civic status. To celebrate, I think I shall go out this morning unto the urban landscape, partake of some brunch and perhaps peruse a newspaper or two.

I may be an urban Indian, but I am also an urbane Indian.

ACTIVITIES

DIRECTLY STATED IDEAS AND INFORMATION

1. List ways in which the author's life is different from the way it was when he grew up.

2. What passages suggest that the author has a good sense of humour and is, perhaps, laughing at himself?

INDIRECTLY STATED IDEAS AND INFORMATION

3. How do you think the author feels about his life now? What gives you this impression?

4. In what ways has the author proven that he is indeed "urbane"?

MAKING CONNECTIONS

5. The author says that after "18 years growing up in that rural community...., [t]he reserve is still deep within me." Reflect upon what aspects of your first eighteen years will always stay with you.

WRITING EXTENSION

Write a paragraph describing how you feel about where you come from. Begin by brainstorming a list of words that describe your background or community.

READING STRATEGY

As you read this poem, stop and visualize the place the narrator is describing.

VOCABULARY PREVIEW

◆ reserve

◆ rhythms

◆ basking

I Grew Up

❖ by Lenore Keeshig-Tobias

i grew up on the reserve
thinking it was the most
beautiful place in the world

i grew up thinking
"i'm never going
to leave this place"

i was a child
a child who would
lie under trees

watching the wind's rhythms
sway leafy boughs
back and forth

back and forth
sweeping it seemed
the clouds into great piles

and rocking me as
i snuggled in the grass
like a bug basking in the sun

i grew up on the reserve
thinking it was the most
beautiful place in the world

i grew up thinking
"i'm never going
to leave this place"

i was a child
a child who ran
wild rhythms

through the fields
the streams
the bush

eating berries
cupping cool water
to my wild stained mouth

and hiding in the
treetops with
my friends

we used to laugh at teachers
and tourists who referred to
our bush as "forest" or "woods"

"forests" or "woods"
were places of
fairytale text

were places where people,
especially children, got lost
where wild beasts roamed

our bush was where we played
and where the rabbits squirrels
foxes deer and the bear lived

i grew up thinking
"i'm never going to
leave this place"

i grew up on the reserve
thinking it was the most
beautiful place in the world

ACTIVITIES

DIRECTLY STATED IDEAS AND INFORMATION

1. List some of the aspects of this narrator's home that made it seem beautiful to her.

2. What clues are there that this narrator felt very free as she was growing up?

INDIRECTLY STATED IDEAS AND INFORMATION

3. How did outsiders (teachers and tourists) see the place where the narrator grew up?

4. Do you think that the narrator has left the reserve? Why or why not?

MAKING CONNECTIONS

5. Think of a place where you have felt very free, and describe what gave you this feeling of freedom.

WRITING EXTENSION

Write a summary of the narrator's experience growing up, using key words and evidence from the poem.

READING STRATEGY
Before you read this selection, look at the title. Make a web with "suitcase lady" written in the middle. Then brainstorm words and ideas you associate with the term. What do you think the article will be about?

VOCABULARY PREVIEW

- ◆ vicomtesse
- ◆ scrounging
- ◆ compassion
- ◆ concerto
- ◆ tiara

Suitcase Lady

❖ by Christie McLaren

Night after night, the woman with the red hair and the purple dress sits in the harsh light of a 24-hour doughnut shop on Queen Street West.

Somewhere in her bleary eyes and in the deep lines of her face is a story that probably no one will ever really know. She is taking pains to write something on a notepad and crying steadily.

She calls herself Vicomtesse Antonia The Linds'ays. She's the suitcase lady of Queen Street.

No one knows how many women there are like her in Toronto. They carry their belongings in shopping bags and spend their days and nights scrounging for food. They have no one and nowhere to go.

This night, in a warm corner with a pot of tea and a pack of Player's, the Vicomtesse is in a mood to talk.

Out of her past come a few scraps: a mother named Savaria; the child of a poor family in Montreal; a brief marriage when she was 20; a son in Toronto who is now 40. "We never got along well because I didn't

bring him up. I was too poor. He never call me mama."

She looks out the window. She's 60 years old.

With her words she spins herself a cocoon. She talks about drapes and carpets, castles and kings. She often lapses into French. She lets her tea get cold. Her hands are big, rough, farmer's hands. How she ended up in the doughnut shop remains a mystery, maybe even to her.

"Before, I had a kitchen and a room and my own furniture. I had to leave everything and go."

It's two years that she's been on the go, since the rooming houses stopped taking her. "I don't have no place to stay."

So she walks. A sturdy coat covers her dress and worn leather boots are on her feet. But her big legs are bare and chapped and she has a ragged cough.

Yes, she says, her legs get tired. She has swollen ankles and, with no socks in her boots, she has blisters. She says she has socks—in the suitcase—but they make her feet itch.

As for money, "I bum on the street. I don't like it, but I have to. I have to survive. The only pleasure I got is my cigarette." She lights another one. "It's not a life."

She recalls the Saturday, a long time ago, when she made $27, and laughs when she tells about how she had to make the money last through Sunday, too: Now she gets "maybe $7 or $8," and eats "very poor."

When she is asked how people treat her, the answer is very matter-of-fact: "Some give money. Some are very polite and some are rude."

In warm weather, she passes her time at the big square in front of City Hall. When it's cold she takes her suitcase west to the doughnut shop.

The waitresses who bring food to the woman look upon her with compassion. They persuaded their boss that her sitting does no harm.

Where does she sleep? "Any place I can find a place to sleep. In the park, in stores . . . like here I stay and sit, on Yonge Street." She shrugs. Sometimes she goes into an underground parking garage.

She doesn't look like she knows what sleep is. "This week I sleep three hours in four days. I feel tired but I wash my face with cold water and I feel okay." Some questions make her eyes turn from the window and stare hard. Then they well over with tears. Like the one about loneliness. "I don't talk much to people," she answers. "Just the elderly, sometimes, in the park."

Her suitcase is full of dreams.

Carefully, she unzips it and pulls out a sheaf of papers—"my concertos."

Each page is crammed with neatly written musical notes—the careful writing she does on the doughnut shop table—but the bar lines are missing. Questions about missing bar lines she tosses aside. Each "concerto" has a French name—Tresor, La Tempete, Le Retour—and each one bears the signature of the Vicomtesse. She smiles and points to one. "A very lovely piece of music. I like it."

She digs in her suitcase again, almost shyly, and produces a round plastic box. Out of it emerges a tiara. Like a little girl, she smooths back her dirty hair and proudly puts it on. No one in the doughnut shop seems to notice.

She cares passionately about the young, the old, and the ones who suffer. So who takes care of the suitcase lady?

"God takes care of me, that's for sure," she says, nodding thoughtfully. "But I'm not what you call crazy about religion. I believe always try to do the best to help people—the elderly, and kids, and my country, and my city of Toronto, Ontario.

ACTIVITIES

DIRECTLY STATED IDEAS AND INFORMATION

1. Reread the first three paragraphs. What would a casual observer notice about this woman?

2. As she talks with the reporter, what background details about the woman's life do we learn? Use sticky notes as you re-read to list these details.

INDIRECTLY STATED IDEAS AND INFORMATION

3. How do the waitresses treat her? Suggest why they treat her this way.

4. What does the writer mean when she says in paragraph 8, "With her words she spins herself a cocoon"?

MAKING CONNECTIONS

5. Have you ever passed someone on the street and wondered what their life experience has been? Describe your impressions of someone you do not know but see regularly around your neighbourhood.

WRITING EXTENSION

Is the problem of homelessness an individual problem or a community problem? Who is responsible? Explain your opinion in a paragraph. Be sure to give reasons for your answer.

READING STRATEGY
*This story is organized into chunks. After you finish each "chunk," **summarize** what has happened and **predict** what might happen next.*

VOCABULARY PREVIEW

◆ gangly
◆ sensuality
◆ torrid
◆ bunting
◆ resin
◆ decrepit
◆ dilapidated
◆ marinade
◆ lacquered
◆ obnoxious
◆ pyromaniac
◆ charade

The "Scream" School of Parenting

❖ by William Bell

I'm thinking of starting a Losers' Club at our school. I'll be president, secretary and membership co-ordinator, all wrapped up in one. I'll let in gangly, zit-speckled boys whose legs and arms have grown faster than their bodies (not to mention their brains), whose Adam's apples bob like golf balls, whose voices moan like cellos one minute and screech like cats the next. You know the ones I mean. They lean against the gym walls at dances, making sarcastic, sexist remarks and think that farts are funny. The females I accept will be like me, girls who hate their hair, who always feel they've chosen the wrong clothes for the day, who have no boyfriends, no boobs (maybe our first meeting will be about whether there's a connection), no life.

Okay, I'm feeling down. Way down. I just came from a Drama Club meeting where I found out I didn't get the part I auditioned for, again. This time it was Blanche in *A Streetcar Named Desire*. The drama teacher, Ms. Cummings, a dumpy, mousy-haired hag who wouldn't know a good actor if she tripped over one, told me I missed the part because I hadn't mastered the "Nawlins" accent.

Really, that's the way she says "New Orleans." As if she's ever been there. The real reason is because I'm small (Mom says "petite") and skinny (Mom says "slender") and my chest isn't noticeable from the audience (Mom says nothing). Cummings rattled on for days before the auditions about how she'd be looking for actors who can develop sexual tension. "You have to drip sensuality," she urged. "This is Nawlins; this the South—hot jazz, torrid, sweaty nights, passion," blah, blah, blah. I felt like saying, You try to pulse with sexual tension when you're almost sixteen and a boy hasn't looked at you in years and you've got a body like a rake handle.

Ah, who cares. It's my birthday and I'm going home to get dinner ready. I hope Mom and Dad make it home on time.

I climb the curved staircase, trailing my hand on the oak bannister, pad down the corridor to my room and toss my backpack on my desk. My CDs have been put away, my clothes hung in the walk-in closet. The bed has been made up, my TV and VCR and stereo dusted. I hate this. The cleaning lady has been in here again. I've asked Mom a million times to tell Audrey to stay out of my room.

I close the door and strip down to my underwear, tossing my clothes over my shoulder onto the carpet—take that, Audrey. I stand before the full-length mirror. What a disaster. Wheat-coloured hair. A plain, thin-lipped face, like the "before" picture in a makeup ad. A body straight and boring as a throughway.

"Naomi, I hate you! You're so deliciously thin," Gillian bubbled the other day as we were dressing for gym. "You could be a model!"

"For what?" I wanted to ask. "A Feed-the-Children campaign? Gardening clothes?"

In my shower, as the hot needles of water prickle my skin, I wonder if I'll feel different tomorrow. Some of my friends make a big deal about turning sixteen, but to me the only positive thing is that I'll be taking my learner's permit test soon. Dad promised to buy me a car when I get my permanent licence next year. That'll be great; I won't be trapped in an empty house any more. If only I had somewhere interesting to go. Or someone to go with.

I put the three steaks I took out of the freezer this morning in some marinade and set them aside. I'm planning my birthday dinner for six o'clock, so I have time to make a tossed green salad and prepare three big potatoes to be nuked in the microwave. To save time, I hung some bunting paper around the kitchen last night. Just as I'm taking off my apron, the phone rings. "I'm running a bit late, darling, but I'm pretty sure I'll be home on time," Mom says, breathless as usual. I can tell from the hollow rumbling in the background that she's calling from her car.

With my preparations done, I pop a can of cola and take it out onto the deck off the kitchen to enjoy the last warm rays of the sun. The planks smell of sawdust and resin and wood stain. Our house, situated on three partially wooded acres, is brand-new, designed and built by my father. It's very secluded—except for the decrepit houses behind us that were supposed to have been torn down a year ago to make way for a golf course. Dad and the country-club developers have been in civil court time after time. The owner of the old houses wants the tenants out but they keep getting delays. Dad's furious, calls them no-goods and welfare bums, taking him to court on free legal aid while he has to shell out real money for his lawyer. (He ought to hire my mother, but she's too busy.) He sank a fortune into our house but the view out the back, which should have included stands of young trees, streams and emerald fairways, is still a rural slum.

There are two semi-detached brick boxes. One stands empty, waiting for the wrecking ball. The second contains two families. Behind the deserted building a dilapidated shed slumps in the yard, along with an ancient Buick sagging on concrete blocks, two broken motorcycles with flat tires and, believe it or not, an asphalt-paving machine. The other yard is graced with a teetering pile of used lumber, two wheelbarrows without the wheels, a dog house without a dog and a yellow snowmobile seamed with rust.

There are three pre-schoolers, two boys and a girl, playing in this yard, yelling at each other at the top of their lungs as they pull a wagonload of stones across the bare, hard-packed ground. "IT'S MY TURN!" "IS NOT!" "I'M TELLING!"—that sort of stuff. These kids learned to communicate from the adults in the house—there seem to be about four or five of them—who are honour graduates of the "Scream" School of Parenting. They shout, holler, bellow, whoop and bawl at each other as if deafness was in their genes. Right now, for instance, the mother is sitting by the kitchen window. I can see the smoke from her cigarette curling up through the screen.

"YOU STOP THAT RIGHT NOW!" she hollers.

"WE'RE NOT DOIN' NOTHIN'."

"I'M TELLING YOU, STOP FIGHTING! AND SHUT UP YER DAMN YELLIN' OR I'M COMIN' OUT THERE!"

"I DON'T CARE!"

She doesn't come out. She's too lazy to haul her carcass off her chair.

"I'M GONNA COUNT TO THREE. THEN I'M COMIN' AFTER YIZ! ONE!"

The three brats ignore her.

"TWO!"

"THREE!" I almost yell, just to end the racket, but the kids continue to scream at each other until the girl takes a rock from the wagon and bounces it off the head of one of the boys. The other boy laughs. The screaming intensifies as I get up and step through the patio door into the kitchen. So much for country relaxation.

It's six-thirty and Dad is still at the construction site. He hasn't even checked in yet. I'm watching a sitcom re-run in the family room when Mom charges through the front door.

"Hello, Naomi!" she trills. Even after a day of phone calls, meetings, tension and deals—she's a lawyer in one of the big firms in the city—she looks attractive, stylishly dressed, her makeup and jewellery understated. Too bad I didn't inherit her looks. She plunks her briefcase down on an empty chair.

"Happy birthday, darling!"

"Thanks, Mom."

"Has your dad called?"

As the word "no" forms in my mouth, the telephone rings.

"Hi, honey. I'm just leaving the site now," he says. "See you in fifteen."

In the kitchen, I remove the salad from the fridge and put it on the table, then take out the steaks. Mom is perched on a bar stool at the counter across from me. I wipe the marinade off the steaks and lay them on a platter. Mom is fidgeting, tapping her lacquered nails on the side of her highball glass.

"How was school today?" she asks as she opens her appointment diary.

"Not so good." It's clear she's forgotten about the audition. "I didn't get the part, just in case you're wondering."

"That's a shame, darling. I'm sorry, I know you worked hard on it." She takes a sip of her rye and ginger. "So who's going to play Ann?"

"That was last year, Mom. This year it's *Streetcar*. Sarah Taylor got the part I was after—Blanche."

"Oh, well. Sarah's a nice girl."

Nice if you like stuck-up and obnoxious.

A chirrupy noise comes from Mom's jacket pocket. She takes out her phone and flips it open.

"Yes? Yes. I—Oh. God I was afraid of that. Yes—"

While she talks I step out to the deck and pull the tarp off the barbecue. One of the adult-male screamers in the other yard is squirting lighter fluid on some balled up papers and bits of wood piled on a hibachi that's balanced on the end of a picnic table. He seems to be the dominant male of the household—a late-middle-aged scarecrow with stringy grey hair held out of his face by a dirty baseball cap, a gaunt face grizzled with a few days' growth. With a loud poof the fire bursts up from his barbecue, forcing him back. He takes a pull on his beer and stares at the smoky fire as if he's never seen flames before.

Starting our barbecue is a matter of turning the valve on the tank, switching on the dials and pushing a red button. Pop! goes

the blue flame. I adjust the dials, lower the lid to let the heat build
up and go back inside just as the scarecrow begins to bellow at the
kids, who are digging a hole beside the snowmobile.

Mom flips her phone closed and puts it down next to her
empty glass, frowning.

"What's up, Mom?"

If you're the daughter of a lawyer you have to be able to keep
secrets. Mom knows I never ever pass on what she tells me about
her cases.

"It's the nursing home action. It looks like we're going to
lose—the first round anyway. Jack is with their lawyers now,
trying to work out a settlement."

The Red Pines Retirement Community on the other side of
town always seems to be in trouble for code violations. The firm
Mom works for represents Red Pines. Her phone, a little thing,
blue with a stubby black antenna, chirps again.

"Yes? Uh-huh. No, no way we'll agree to that. They're bluffing.
No, I can't, not yet. Maybe later. I'll call you."

She flips it closed. "I think I'll take a shower and get into
something fresh," she says, slipping off the stool.

In the other yard, my pyromaniac neighbour seems to
have his fire under control. He has been joined by the dumpy
woman, another cigarette dangling from her mouth, and two
men. The four of them are sitting on kitchen chairs on their
porch, drinking beer from bottles and discussing something
with a lot of energy. Occasionally, a burst of laughter punches
into our kitchen.

I'm tossing oil and vinegar dressing into the salad when Dad
bursts in.

"Hi, kiddo, how's it going?"

My father doesn't look like a builder. He's small for a man—
"Not short, on the lower end of average," he says—slim, with
black hair and rugged features. He takes his phone—wood-grain
finish, very appropriate—from the pouch on his belt and puts
it on the countertop beside Mom's, then pulls an imported lager
from the fridge and pours it carefully into a long, tapered glass.

"What a day," he sighs, a moustache of white foam over his lip. "Sometimes I wonder if those idiots can spell the word 'schedule,' never mind keep one."

He wipes away the foam with the back of his hand. "How's things with the smartest kid at Woodlawn High?"

"Okay, I guess." I wait, but he doesn't ask. "I didn't get the part," I tell him. "Blanche, in *Streetcar*."

"Shoot. I know you wanted that one badly. Oh, well, there will be other roles."

Maybe so, but I won't get them. I'm obviously going to go through life playing walk-ons. The microwave beeps, and I jab each potato with a fork to make sure it's done.

"I'm going to put the steaks on now, Dad, okay?"

"Great. I'm hungry as a wolf."

I take the platter of meat outside and slap the steaks on the hot grill, where they immediately begin to hiss and splutter, then set my watch for two minutes.

"HATTIE, I TOLD YOU TO LEAVE HIM ALONE!"

"I DIDN'T TOUCH HIM!"

"YES YOU DID; I SAW YOU. STOP THE DAMN LYIN'."

"YOU'RE THE LIAR, NOT ME."

"WATCH YOUR TONGUE, MY GIRL, OR I'M COMIN' DOWN THERE AND WHACK YOU A GOOD ONE."

"BETCHA WON'T!"

The kid knows what she's talking about. The adults holler threats but remain parked in their chairs. Only a nuclear blast would budge them. Or a drained beer bottle. My watch beeps and I turn over the steaks and set the timer again.

Scarecrow is flipping hamburgers in a cloud of smoke. "SANDY, BRING OUT SOME MORE BEER WITH THE POTATOES."

"ALL RIGHT, ALL RIGHT," comes a muffled female voice from the house. "I ONLY GOT TWO HANDS, YOU KNOW. ONE OF YIZ COULD SET THE TABLE."

I lift the steaks off the grill with the tongs and turn off the barbecue, then carry the platter inside, slamming the patio door behind me.

At the table, Mom and Dad look anything but relaxed as they cut into their steaks.

"This is delicious, kiddo," Dad offers. "Best steak I've ever—"

A phone chirps. Both Mom and Dad look at the countertop where the two phones rest like little soldiers, ready for action.

"Do you think we could possibly get through my birthday dinner without your little friends over there?" I ask my parents.

"It's mine," Mom says, standing and snatching up the blue one. "Yes?"

"So are there any other parts in the play you can get?"

"Okay, that's a bit more reasonable."

"Not really. Dad. It's basically a three-hander."

"Oh, I've never seen that play. Never liked O'Neill."

"No, we won't budge on that point. We can't."

"It's Williams, Dad."

"Oh, yeah, right."

Mom sits down again. "I'm sorry, Naomi, but I'm going to have to go out later."

"Aw, Mom, it's my birthday. I rented a video and everything, that French flick you guys were talking about last week."

"I know, dear, but it can't be helped. I've got to be there; the whole thing's falling apart."

We eat in silence for a few moments. I'm doing a slow burn, wondering why I bothered to go ahead with this charade of a birthday party to begin with, but no one seems to notice. As if on cue, a phone squeaks.

"My turn, I guess," Dad says. Then, into the phone, "Magee here."

"I'll try to be back as quickly as I can, darling."

"What do you mean the insulation won't be there in the morning? They promised."

"Can we watch the video later, Mom?"

"Sure, that will be fine. I'm looking forward to it."

"But we can't proceed until the drywall comes. I was hoping to get it up and taped tomorrow."

"Okay. I guess I could work on my project until then."

"Oh, hell, you really think I need to come over there?"

"Is that the essay on teenage alienation?"

"No, I handed that in long ago. Got an A, too."

"Wonderful, I'm proud of you."

Dad plunks himself down in his chair. "I've got to slip out for a half hour or so after dinner."

Mom frowns. "Well, why don't you open your gift now, dear, just in case we're held up?"

The other yard is lit by a spotlight dangling from the clothesline pole. The whole bunch of them are munching hamburgers, sloshing down the beer, yakking and laughing. I sit on our deck in the dark, holding my gift in my lap. It's a portable CD player, pink-pearl finish, with lots of buttons—all the features. It's expensive, a real gem.

The colour is different, but it's the same model Mom and Dad bought me for Christmas five months ago.

I hold it in my lap, my fingers caressing the smooth plastic. In the other yard, somebody turns on a radio.

That is what learning is. You suddenly understand something you've understood all your life, but in a new way.

— *Doris Lessing (b. 1919)*
Writer

ACTIVITIES

DIRECTLY STATED IDEAS AND INFORMATION

1. List in point form all the information that is given about the neighbours in the semi-detached house.

2. What details does the narrator provide about the lifestyle of her own parents?

INDIRECTLY STATED IDEAS AND INFORMATION

3. What sorts of things make the main character in this story feel alienated?

4. What do you think would make Naomi feel very happy on her birthday?

MAKING CONNECTIONS

5. What will you try to do, if you become a parent, in order to connect with your children?

WRITING EXTENSION

Write a letter to either Naomi or her parents in which you share your opinion of the situation and offer some advice.

READING STRATEGY

*Look at the chart on page 115. **Scan** the columns to find out what it is about. As you read, think about how the statistics in the chart are related to those in the text.*

VOCABULARY PREVIEW

◆ census
◆ traditional
◆ proportion
◆ common-law

Canadian Families Changing

❖ by Guenther Zuern

What's a typical Canadian family?

There's no simple answer. Over the past 20 years, Canadian families have changed a lot. Here are some of those changes shown by the 2001 census.

Traditional family

The "traditional" family—married parents with one or more children at home—is declining as a proportion of all families. In 1981, 55 percent of all families were traditional families. In 2001, the figure was down to 41 percent. During the same period, there was an increase in couples without children, single-parent families, and step families.[1] The number of common-law couples also went up.

Common-law couples

Couples living together without being married represent 14 percent of all families. Two decades ago the proportion was only 6 percent. Common-law couples with children are increasing.

Single parents

One quarter of all families with children at home have only one parent. The majority of single parents are women. Single-parent families represent 16 percent of all Canadian families.

Same-sex relationships

The 2001 census was the first to include same-sex relationships within the definition of common-law couples. A total of 34 200 gay and lesbian couples were counted in Canada. This represents 0.5 percent of all families.

Staying with mom and dad

Young adults are living with their parents longer. There are 3.8 million Canadians aged 20 to 29, and 41 percent of them still live in their parents' home.

---

1 "Step family" refers to a family in which at least one of the children in the home is from a previous relationship of one of the parents.

THREE GENERATIONS: Susie Pichelli, second from right, her husband George, right, and their children Michael and Stephanie live with her parents, Anna and Matteo Camillo, in North York, Ontario. According to the 2001 census, only 3 percent of children live in the same home as one or more grandparents.

Home alone

More people than ever are living alone. About one out of every four of the country's 11.5 million households is occupied by just one person. One major reason is the growing number of seniors in Canada. (Seniors are people who are 65 or older.)

Smaller households are the fastest growing type in Canada. The average household size in Canada is 2.6 persons.

FAMILY PORTRAITS

Statistics Canada's 2001 census includes three main components in its definition of a "census family"—married couples, common-law couples (including same-sex couples), and single parents.

Families composed of	*% of all families*
Married couples	70
With children at home	41
Without children at home	29
Common-law couples	14
With children at home	6
Without children at home	8
Single Parents	16

ACTIVITIES

DIRECTLY STATED IDEAS AND INFORMATION

1. What three changes in Canadian families have occurred over the past 20 years?

2. Look at the Family Portraits chart. Which family unit has the highest proportion of children at home?

INDIRECTLY STATED IDEAS AND INFORMATION

3. What does the answer to question 2 tell you about Canadian attitudes towards marriage and children?

4. How do you account for the fact that young adults are staying with their parents longer?

MAKING CONNECTIONS

5. Think about your family, and other families you know, in terms of trends in Canadian families. Are you typical? Why or why not?

WRITING EXTENSION

Write a news report in which you highlight several of the recent trends in Canadian families. Include quotations from representatives of families.

READING STRATEGY

*Try the **wordsplash** strategy. Write your own definition for each of the following: cultural diversity, multiculturalism, nationality, and ethnic origins. Use each term in a sentence that illustrates its meaning. Then read the text, and compare the text definitions with your own. Revise your definitions and write new sentences to illustrate your new understanding of these terms.*

VOCABULARY PREVIEW

◆ Aboriginal
◆ cultural diversity
◆ multiculturalism
◆ generations
◆ ethnic origins

Our Cultural Diversity

❖ by Colin M. Bain

What are your cultural roots? Where did your parents grow up? Your grandparents? Your great-grandparents? For most Canadians, the answer to at least one of these questions is likely to be "somewhere else." That's because, apart from Aboriginal peoples, who are the original occupants of the land, we are all either immigrants, or descended from immigrants.

Canada is a nation that prides itself on its cultural diversity. This term means that the population is drawn from many cultural backgrounds, illustrating a wide range of practices and beliefs. What's more, Canada has an official policy of multiculturalism, which means people are encouraged to retain their cultural heritage while also being committed Canadians. So it is quite normal for many of us to say that we are, for example, "Italian," "Korean," or "Nigerian," even after several generations in this country. As you will see, there are many ways of measuring the cultural diversity of the Canadian people.

Ethnic Origins

Canadians frequently think of themselves in terms of their ethnic origins, or cultural background. Ethnic origins are not always the

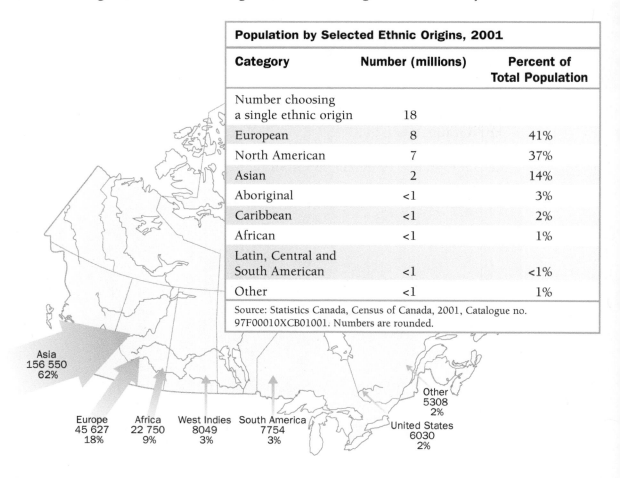

Population by Selected Ethnic Origins, 2001

Category	Number (millions)	Percent of Total Population
Number choosing a single ethnic origin	18	
European	8	41%
North American	7	37%
Asian	2	14%
Aboriginal	<1	3%
Caribbean	<1	2%
African	<1	1%
Latin, Central and South American	<1	<1%
Other	<1	1%

Source: Statistics Canada, Census of Canada, 2001, Catalogue no. 97F00010XCB01001. Numbers are rounded.

Asia
156 550
62%

Europe
45 627
18%

Africa
22 750
9%

West Indies
8049
3%

South America
7754
3%

Other
5308
2%

United States
6030
2%

same as nationality, especially in Canada. Canadian citizens—both those who were born here and those who came as immigrants and took out Canadian citizenship—have the same nationality, but a wide array of ethnic origins.

Canada was once a colony of France. Later, it became a British colony. So it is understandable that many Canadians have European origins. In fact, until the 1970s, most immigrants to Canada came from Europe. Beginning in the 1980s, however, immigrants began to come from many other places. The table on the previous page shows the ethnic origins of Canadians who were already living here in 2001. The map shows where immigrants who came to Canada in 2000–2001 arrived from. See the difference.

ACTIVITIES

DIRECTLY STATED IDEAS AND INFORMATION

1. Why is it understandable that many Canadians trace their ethnic origin back to Europe?

2. Looking at the map, from where did the largest group of immigrants come in 2001?

INDIRECTLY STATED IDEAS AND INFORMATION

3. In the Population by Selected Ethnic Origins chart, where is the second largest group from? What does this statistic mean?

4. Why are so many Canadians considered to be immigrants?

MAKING CONNECTIONS

5. Do a survey of a group in your class. How many people have at least one relative who was born outside of Canada? How many generations back do most people have to go?

WRITING EXTENSION

Write an information paragraph in which you explain how Canada has evolved as a multicultural country. Highlight key points from the information presented, and use your own words to explain these ideas.

READING STRATEGY

This is a story told in a poem. **Skim** *the poem and list the characters mentioned.*

VOCABULARY PREVIEW

◆ motherlove
◆ snugged
◆ curly electric

Reach Out and Touch

❖ by Maxine Tynes

baby girl, baby boy behind me on the bus
reach out
and touch the curly electric of my hair
your fingers dipped in the
brown skin magic of my neck
to see if it comes off
your mama
slapping hands away
hush-up of your questions
and wondering out loud why it doesn't come off.
I turn and smile for you,
But you're already lost
In the silence and the fear that motherlove wraps you in.
I should have sat beside you
snugged up my big warm self up close
held you while your mama juggled parcels.
then you would know it's ok.

ACTIVITIES

DIRECTLY STATED IDEAS AND INFORMATION

1. Explain what the baby was doing, and how the mother reacted.

2. List the words used to describe the mother's response.

INDIRECTLY STATED IDEAS AND INFORMATION

3. What do the words you listed in question 2 make you think about the mother?

4. How does the narrator feel about the child's curiosity?

MAKING CONNECTIONS

5. The mother and the narrator in the poem both respond to the child's curiosity. Reflect on why their responses are so different.

WRITING EXTENSION

What would you like to say to this mother? Express your opinion in a letter.

No act of kindness, no matter how small, is ever wasted.

— *Aesop (620 BC–560 BC)*
Greek Writer

READING STRATEGY

As you read this selection, look for answers to the 5 W's: Who, When, Where, What, Why. Write answers to these questions in note form in your notebook.

VOCABULARY PREVIEW

- order-in-council
- War Measures Act
- warrant
- internment camps
- evacuation
- discrimination
- saboteurs
- detention camps
- deported
- relocation
- forcibly uprooted
- compensation

Japanese Canadians
Wartime Persecution

During the Second World War, all people of Japanese background living on the coast of British Columbia were forced to leave their homes. Why were Japanese Canadians unjustly singled out?

The Relocation Begins

In February 1942, Prime Minister King made a dramatic announcement. By order-in-council, under the War Measures Act, all people of Japanese background living within 62 km of the coast of British Columbia would be moved away from the coast. The RCMP could search their homes without a warrant; there would be no trials or investigations. It did not matter how long people had been living in Canada, or whether or not they were citizens—and many were.

Immediately, authorities began rounding up people of Japanese background. Over the next few months about 20 000 were removed from their homes and taken to internment camps in the interior of B.C.,

where they were forced to live for the rest of the war. Others were sent to work as labourers in the Prairies and Ontario. While they were gone, the federal government took their property and sold it at auctions.

The evacuation was explained as a security precaution. The war with Japan was going badly. At the end of 1941, the Japanese had carried out a surprise air attack on the U.S. naval base at Pearl Harbor in Hawaii. Then they overran much of East Asia. These events convinced people in B.C. that a Japanese invasion was certain. As it turned out, an invasion did not occur, but for many months British Columbians lived in fear that the war would reach their doorstep.

In this situation, it was argued, people of Japanese origin posed a threat. British

This internment camp near Slocan, B.C., was typical of the settlements in which Japanese evacuees were forced to live.

Columbia already had a long history of discrimination against its Chinese, Japanese, and South Asian residents. The war provided an excuse for this prejudice to come bubbling to the surface again. People suspected that Japanese Canadians were more Japanese than Canadian, that they would feel loyalty to their country of origin and become spies and saboteurs on its behalf. There is no evidence that this ever happened, but such was the strength of public prejudice that the government felt it had to give in to it.

As anti-Japanese feelings grew, some people began to fear outbreaks of violence and argued that the Japanese should be moved for their own safety. Since the fall of Hong Kong in December 1941, many Canadian soldiers were prisoners of war in Japanese detention camps. The government worried that if any harm came to Japanese residents in Canada, the Japanese would take revenge on the prisoners.

Apologizing for Injustice

After the war, the persecution of Japanese Canadians continued. For several years they were not allowed to return to the coast. Many were deported back to Japan or sent to live in eastern Canada. At the time, most Canadians approved the relocation of the Japanese. Today, it is recognized as one of the worst violations of human rights in the history of the country. Innocent people, most of them Canadian citizens, were forcibly uprooted and taken from their homes and sent to camps or labour jobs across the country. They lost their possessions and their livelihoods. All of this was done seemingly to preserve national security, which almost everyone now agrees was never at risk.

Japanese Canadians persisted in seeking compensation for all they had suffered. They also wanted the government to admit that an injustice had been done. Finally, in 1988, the government of Canada agreed. It admitted that "the treatment of Japanese Canadians during and after World War II was unjust and violated principles of human rights as they are understood today." It apologized and agreed to pay $21 000 to every evacuee who was still living, as well as other money to the Japanese-Canadian community as a whole.

ACTIVITIES

DIRECTLY STATED IDEAS AND INFORMATION

1. Why was the Canadian government persuaded that people of Japanese background were a threat to security?

2. Describe how Japanese Canadians were treated after the attack on Pearl Harbour.

INDIRECTLY STATED IDEAS AND INFORMATION

3. Why did the Japanese community seek compensation?

4. What is suggested by the phrase "as they are understood today" in the apology?

MAKING CONNECTIONS

5. Reflect upon how you would feel if your government treated you in this way.

WRITING EXTENSION

Many Canadians today are unaware of the internment of Japanese Canadians. Write a newspaper article in which you observe the anniversary of the apology being made by the Canadian government.

READING STRATEGY

*Before you read this selection, copy the **anticipation guide** below into your notebook. Follow the instructions on page 18 to fill in the chart.*

ANTICIPATION GUIDE	ME	TEXT
1. Most teens loiter because they are bored.	___	___
2. Most youth loitering doesn't involve crime.	___	___
3. Adults often feel intimidated by groups of loitering teens.	___	___
4. Teens are often rude to police when they are told not to loiter.	___	___
5. Stopping teens from loitering is a community problem.	___	___

VOCABULARY PREVIEW

- intimidated
- loiters
- notorious
- dissuade
- appropriately
- discretion

Teen Loitering— What the Heck Are They Up To?

❖ by Vijay Narasimhan

In almost any part of town, if you stop at a Tim Hortons between the hours of 10 PM and 2 AM, you're likely to see a pack of kids hanging around in the parking lot. Most adults feel a bit intimidated, and think that these kids are up to no good. Josée caught up with a few of these young people at the Tim Hortons on Innes Road in Ottawa and they told her what was really going down.

"All we want is a place to meet, talk, and laugh," says Justin, a member of this group. "If we hang out in a dark place, people will probably think that we're doing something bad. We have nothing to hide: we're in a well-lit area and everyone can see what we're doing."

But why, you may ask, would people choose to meet at the Tim Hortons? Well, the answer is pretty simple. The kids who hang out here are too young to go to bars and clubs, and too noisy and numerous to hang out at people's houses. "It's understandable that our parents don't want us to stay at home. After all they're tired and need to relax too," says Mark, the youngest of the group.

According to Jeff, a Grade 10 student who loiters from time to time, it's a matter of convenience. "Kids can hang out, talk, eat if they get hungry, and use the bathroom if they have to," he says. Also, with the new smoking by-law in effect, youth can't go to a restaurant for a bite to eat while smoking a cigarette. They have no choice but to meet outside.

As you can see, most youth loitering doesn't involve crime and illegal activity. However, some teens give everyone a bad rap. "If you go out to other Tim Hortons in town, you can see all sorts of stuff," says another member of the Innes Road group. "At some, it's a regular 'car show,' where kids show off their souped-up cars to one another and see who can screech their tires loudest." Other Tim Hortons feature teens that take it even further. Teens meet and then retire to a deserted country road where they race their cars. Still other hangouts are notorious for underage drinking and drug use.

How do local police react to the problem? According to Constable Diana Hampson of the Ottawa Police, the cops receive complaints about loitering almost every weekend during the summer. "Ninety percent of kids will respect the police if they are told not to loiter, but the other 10 percent are really

rude," she remarks. Youth can be charged with trespassing or mischief if they do not comply with the police; being cuffed, charged, and slapped with a considerable fine are probably not the most enjoyable ways to end off a Friday night.

What can be done to dissuade youth from loitering? Just ask Jeff. "You have to react appropriately. If a business feels that youth are intimidating customers, then they have a right to ask them to leave. At the same time, you shouldn't try to get them angry at you, because then they'll cause more trouble." Some businesses have taken after the strategy of a 7-Eleven in Vancouver by playing classical or polka music outside their store to turn off kids who want to stay there for more than just a few minutes. If youth are vandalizing property or causing mischief, employers should most probably call the police. Most people agree that business owners should use their discretion and react to the problem of loitering with a level of action appropriate to what the teens are doing.

Abdul, another teen who sometimes likes to play soccer near a McDonald's restaurant, says that he would rather go to a park than a parking lot; unfortunately, not many are available in his area. Jeff adds that he would much rather play basketball than just sit around, but that courts aren't always within walking distance. It looks like the construction of more recreational facilities, including well-lit basketball courts, skate parks, and soccer fields, are an integral part of reducing the incidence of teen loitering.

One idea that has been extremely successful in different communities is a "youth centre." This establishment is found in a residential area and contains game rooms and lounges where kids can meet up and hang out. The administrator of the facility is also responsible for creating activities in which young people can participate. "The introduction of a youth centre in a community reduces the percentage of loitering significantly," says Constable Hampson. It offers all of the "convenience" of a Tim Hortons while providing youth with ample opportunities to actually do something.

Truth be told, teens loiter because they are bored. Although businesses should take the necessary action to prevent loitering on their premises, it is up to the greater community to get youth more involved in order to keep them out of parking lots.

ACTIVITIES

DIRECTLY STATED IDEAS AND INFORMATION

1. What is the age group of young people most likely to loiter?

2. What are some strategies businesses have used to prevent teens from loitering?

INDIRECTLY STATED IDEAS AND INFORMATION

3. Explain why adults might feel intimidated by teen loitering.

4. According to this selection, what are some reasons that young people would choose to hang out at Tim Hortons?

MAKING CONNECTIONS

5. According to this selection and your own ideas, explain whether teens who are loitering are "up to no good."

WRITING EXTENSION

In a minimum of three paragraphs, write an opinion piece that answers the question, "Should the greater community be responsible for getting young people more involved to prevent loitering?" State your point of view in the first paragraph, and back it up with reasons, examples, or facts in the next two paragraphs.

READING STRATEGY

*Use a **discussion web** for this selection. Copy the following chart into your notebook. As you read, fill in the two sides of the chart in point form with reasons given in the text.*

Yes	Should students have to wait until age 18 to get a driver's licence?	No

VOCABULARY PREVIEW

- ◆ frustrated
- ◆ convenient
- ◆ caution
- ◆ advocate
- ◆ capabilities
- ◆ rationally
- ◆ abided

To Drive or Not To Drive

Dear Jean:

I am 16 years old, and I have my driver's permit. I am also trying to get a job for the summer. My mother will not allow me to practise driving, and she says I will not be allowed to get my licence until I am 18. I am frustrated about this, since I am at the age where most of my friends are driving, and it would be more convenient for me if I could drive myself to work. I know my mother doesn't trust me, but she really has no reason not to. She hasn't even given me a chance! How can I express my frustration and help her to realize the importance of my getting my licence without her getting angry and snapping at me about it?

Jean responds:

Hi,

Thanks for writing to parentingadolescents.com.

I can understand your frustration at your mother's caution around your driving at 16. Not only would it be more convenient for you, as you say, to drive to work, but also getting your driver's licence is seen as a kind of "rite of passage" in the culture, and the age has been set at 16 for some kind of reason, so it's hard to have a parent who is apparently more cautious than the average.

I guess you can't help but feel that your mom doesn't trust you, but you know, it's just possible that something else is involved. For instance, the major cause of death and injuries among young people is automobile accidents. That's a very sobering statistic for parents to deal with! Perhaps your mom feels that the age is set too young in the society generally; maybe she'd advocate for making the age of driving 18 or above for everyone, not just for you.

We now know that the adolescent brain is still developing, right through adolescence, and that's not the view we used to have. We used to think basically all of the adult traits were "in" the brain by age 13 or even earlier. My point is that adolescents do not yet possess all of the capabilities and skills that they will possess when they're past 21. While teens are actually better than adults at some things, their social and emotional development is still going on, so they are not yet prepared to make mature judgments in the more difficult areas, and they tend still to be driven by their emotions. The latter quality could mean real trouble on the road, as you may imagine.

So, as a parent, perhaps your mom is thinking of some of these things when she says no driving until you're 18. Perhaps, in other words, she's just trying to save your life!

On the other hand, she cannot protect you from all dangers, no matter what she does, and you could be as easily hurt by a friend in whose car you might be riding, as by an accident you could get into when you yourself were driving.

I think the only hope of helping your mom change her mind is to talk to her as calmly and rationally as you can. You might ask her to tell you her reasons, when the two of you are both feeling good, so you can understand where she's coming from. Really listen to what she says and give her the benefit of the doubt. Then, ask her what, if anything, would make her feel more comfortable about allowing you to drive sooner than 18. . . . Is there any rule or any provision that would make her feel less frightened about your safety? What if, for example, you had extended practice—more than is strictly required for getting your licence, perhaps with a professional instructor? What if you abided by a rule that said that you could not drive friends your own age in the car (I know that's harsh, but you're bargaining here for something your mom can grant or withhold, and you most likely will not get everything you want)?

This might relieve her mind about your getting emotionally overstimulated by friends and making a mistake on the road. What if you yourself actually obtained the statistics about the cause of accidents for young people and discussed them with your mom?—because, as I recall them, the numbers indicate that there is a high rate of accidents into the early 20s, so it's more a matter of individual safe practices than age *per se*. To find the stats, start with **www.youthwork.com/generalstats.html**.

Another possibility you might want to explore is engaging with your mother in the "I Promise" program, in which the car you will drive is labelled with a phone number observers can call if you are driving dangerously. (Note that both teen and parent promise to drive safely, in this program.)

Good luck. . . . You can't "make" her see or understand anything, but if you talk with her like an adult, she's much more likely to feel that you have developed your judgment to the place where maybe you could be trusted to drive a car, than if you complain and cry to her like a kid.

P.S. Re your mother's becoming angry and "snapping" at you: again, the tone with which you approach her may make a difference. It's also possible that your mom needs to remember not to "make you wrong" for asking for something that she's not yet ready to grant. "Everyone gets to make a request; everyone is free to grant or deny the request"—that's a principle of "assertiveness" training that may come in handy.

— Jean

ACTIVITIES

DIRECTLY STATED IDEAS AND INFORMATION

1. According to this selection, what tends to drive the judgment of teenagers?

2. What is the major cause of death and injuries among young people?

INDIRECTLY STATED IDEAS AND INFORMATION

3. What is meant by the phrase "rite of passage" as it is used in this selection?

4. To whom is this teenager writing?

MAKING CONNECTIONS

5. According to this selection and your own ideas, explain why the mother of the teen writing the letter might not want her daughter to drive until she is 18 years old.

WRITING EXTENSION

Write a letter to the editor on the topic "Should the driving age be raised to age 18?" Make sure you choose one side of the debate and provide details to support it.

READING STRATEGY

*Before you look at this selection in detail, **skim** it to get a general idea of what it's about and to see how many signs you recognize.*

VOCABULARY PREVIEW

- ◆ uneven
- ◆ steep
- ◆ caution
- ◆ pedestrians
- ◆ temporary
- ◆ detour
- ◆ milled
- ◆ traction

Traffic Signs

1. Signs

 Traffic lights ahead. Slow down.

 Snowmobiles cross this road.

 Bump or uneven pavement on the road ahead. Slow down and keep control of your vehicle.

 Steep hill ahead. You may need to use a lower gear.

 Traffic travels in both directions on the same road ahead. Keep to the right.

 Railway crossing ahead. Be alert for trains. This sign also shows the angle at which the railway tracks cross the road.

 Two roads going in the same direction are about to join into one. Drivers on both are equally responsible for seeing that traffic merges smoothly and safely.

 Underpass ahead. Take care if you are driving a tall vehicle. Sign shows how much room you have.

 Sharp turn or bend in the road in the direction of the arrow. The checker-board border warns of danger. Slow down; be careful.

Deer regularly cross this road; be alert for animals.

 Watch for pedestrians and be prepared to share the road with them.

 This sign warns you that you are coming to a hidden school bus stop. Slow down, drive with extra caution, watch for children and for a school bus with flashing red lights.

 Truck entrance on the right side of the road ahead. If the sign shows the truck on the left, the entrance is on the left side of the road.

 Watch for fallen rock and be prepared to avoid a collision.

 These signs warn of a school crossing. Watch for children and follow the directions of the crossing guard or school safety patroller.

 Shows maximum safe speed on ramp.

 There may be water flowing over the road.

Temporary condition signs

These signs warn of unusual temporary conditions such as road work zones, diversions, detours, lane closures, or traffic control people on the road. They are usually diamond shaped with an orange background and black letters or symbols.

Here are some common temporary condition signs:

 Survey crew working on the road ahead.

 Temporary detour from normal traffic route.

 Traffic control person ahead. Drive slowly and watch for instructions.

 Flashing lights on the arrow show the direction to follow.

 Construction work one kilometre ahead.

 You are entering a construction zone. Drive with extra caution and be prepared for a lower speed limit.

 Road work ahead.

Pavement has been milled or grooved. Your vehicle's stopping ability may be affected so obey the speed limit and drive with extra caution. Motorcyclists may experience reduced traction on these surfaces.

 Closed lane. Adjust speed to merge with traffic in lane indicated by arrow.

 Lane ahead is closed for roadwork. Obey the speed limit and merge with traffic in the open lane.

 Reduce speed and be prepared to stop.

 Do not pass the pilot or pace vehicle bearing this sign.

ACTIVITIES

DIRECTLY STATED IDEAS AND INFORMATION

1. On the underpass sign on the first page, how much room do vehicles have under the underpass?

2. Why does a driver need to be careful when driving on milled or grooved pavement?

INDIRECTLY STATED IDEAS AND INFORMATION

3. Look at the signs on the last page of the selection. What do you think the manual is referring to when it mentions a "pilot" or "pace" vehicle?

4. Why would a driver need to know that a survey crew is working on the road ahead?

MAKING CONNECTIONS

5. According to this selection and your own ideas, explain the overall purpose of traffic signs.

WRITING EXTENSION

Write a list of at least six point-form rules for new drivers to help them drive safely. You may use your own experience as well as information from the selection.

READING STRATEGY

*Write the question, "Does the insurance industry discriminate against young males?" at the top of your page. Underneath, create a **T-chart** with the left-hand column titled "Yes" and the right-hand column titled "No." Fill in the chart as you are reading this selection.*

VOCABULARY PREVIEW

- staggering
- unprecedented
- discrimination
- demographics
- premiums
- arbitrary

The Globe and Mail   Monday, June 23, 2003

Rising Car Insurance Hits Young Men Hardest

❖ by Peter Cheney and Paul Waldie

For Tony Roeding, living at home while he went to Saint Mary's University looked like the perfect plan—at least until he found out that insurance for the used Honda he planned to commute with would cost $6000.

"I couldn't believe it," said Mr. Roeding, who recently turned 20. "It was one of the most ridiculous things I ever heard. The car only cost $10 000, and they wanted more than half that."

Mr. Roeding, who lives near Peggy's Cove, N.S., is one of countless young Canadian men who have found themselves hit with staggering car insurance bills that have forced them to adjust their plans by working harder, moving, or even giving up on driving altogether.

Their woes are part of a national crisis that has jacked up the cost of insurance to unprecedented levels for many Canadians. Many drivers in Atlantic Canada, for example, have seen increases of 60 to 70 percent. In Ontario, rates have jumped as much as 25 percent.

"The system is a mess," said Stephen Boyce of the New Brunswick Consumers' Coalition. "I don't think it's working for anybody."

Although most Canadian drivers have seen increases, young male drivers have been hit particularly hard. Industry experts say it's now common for 18-year-olds to pay $8000 to insure a used car. One 19-year-old Toronto man with a clean driving record, for example, was recently quoted $9000 to insure his used car.

Although young men have long paid far more for insurance than other drivers, since they are considered higher risks, some have begun to challenge the logic that pushes their rates so high. Mr. Roeding, for example, believes that the insurance industry's rating system is a form of discrimination.

"It seems like this is the only area of life where you're allowed to discriminate," he said. "I get judged because I'm a member of a group, not because of who I actually am. That's what discrimination is, and it's supposed to be illegal."

Mr. Roeding notes that a female cousin whose demographics are virtually identical to his own pays a small fraction of what he does. "What makes her different?" he asked. "Why are they allowed to charge me so much just because I'm a male? They aren't allowed to look at other groups in the same way. What if they decided that members of some racial groups had more accidents? Would they be allowed to charge every member of the group more because of that?"

Mr. Roeding believes the only fair way to judge drivers is by assessing their actual driving records. By that standard,

Mr. Roeding would appear to be a good risk. He has been driving since he was 16, lives in a low-traffic area, attended a Young Drivers of Canada course, and has no tickets or accidents. A more careful examination shows other positive factors, including the guidance of his father, a retired fighter pilot who recently served as the base safety officer for Canadian Forces Base Shearwater.

"I'm a careful driver," Mr. Roeding said. "But I get judged just because of the group I'm in."

Mr. Roeding's case is typical of young drivers who live in provinces that are served by private auto insurance.

The situation is far different in provinces such as British Columbia and Manitoba. Their public systems use different rating criteria.

Brandon Sparks, 17, who lives in Abbotsford, B.C., for example, pays just $1740 a year to insure his 1988 Honda Civic, far less than young men in Ontario or Atlantic Canada would pay. Nick Geer, chief executive officer of Insurance Corp. of British Columbia (ICBC), said the government-run insurer does not discriminate on the basis of age in setting rates.

"We don't differentiate on age, sex, or marital status," Mr. Geer said. "You have to buy into a discount and have accident-free years."

The provincially owned corporation has kept premiums and rate increases below the national average. But others say not taking age or sex into account raises other issues of discrimination. Ryan Lee, a business professor at the University of Calgary who has studied auto insurance, says female ICBC customers probably pay more than they should because of the artificially low rates charged to young males.

Steve Smith, vice-president of Kingsway Financial Services, an Ontario-based insurer, rejects the notion that the high rates charged to young men are discriminatory.

"It isn't arbitrary," he said. "It's based on statistics. You can't argue with it."

Mr. Smith said his company's rating system is typical of the private insurance industry. It takes into account a number of factors that include sex, age, location, marital status, and driving experience. An 18-year-old man, Mr. Smith said, typically pays four to five times as much as a married 45-year-old.

Gary Direnfeld, an Ontario social worker who started a safe-driving program for teenagers called I Promise, also rejects the idea that high rates discriminate against young males.

"The statistics are clear," he said. "Young men have more crashes. And the only thing you can do is judge them as a group, because as individuals they don't have enough driving history yet. It's unfortunate, but that's the way it is."

Mr. Direnfeld said car crashes involving teenage drivers cause about 6000 deaths and 400 000 injuries in North America each year. He estimates the cost of these crashes to the insurance industry at $32.8 billion. The vast majority are caused by young male drivers, Mr. Direnfeld said.

"They're the ones at fault," he said. "Open any newspaper and you'll see the proof. And the statistics back it up." ■

I think of a hero as someone who understands the degree of responsibility that comes with his freedom.

— *Bob Dylan (b. 1941)*
Singer and Songwriter

ACTIVITIES

DIRECTLY STATED IDEAS AND INFORMATION

1. What factors does the private insurance industry take into account when determining insurance rates?

2. According to the text, how many injuries are caused by teenage drivers in North America each year?

INDIRECTLY STATED IDEAS AND INFORMATION

3. Explain why Tony Roeding feels he's being discriminated against.

4. Explain why some people believe that female car insurance customers in British Columbia pay more than they should for insurance.

MAKING CONNECTIONS

5. Have you been affected by the cost of automobile insurance? If so, explain how. If not, interview someone who has been affected to find out how they have coped.

WRITING EXTENSION

Should young males pay more for insurance than females and other age groups? Present your opinion in a well-developed opinion piece. Use information from the text and your own experience to support your ideas.

READING STRATEGY

Skim *over the entire graph to get a sense of what it is about. Start with the title. Then look at each axis on the graph to see what it represents. Check the colour key below the graph. As you look at the bars, think about how you would express what you are seeing in words.*

VOCABULARY PREVIEW

◆ profile

◆ median

Insurance Rates

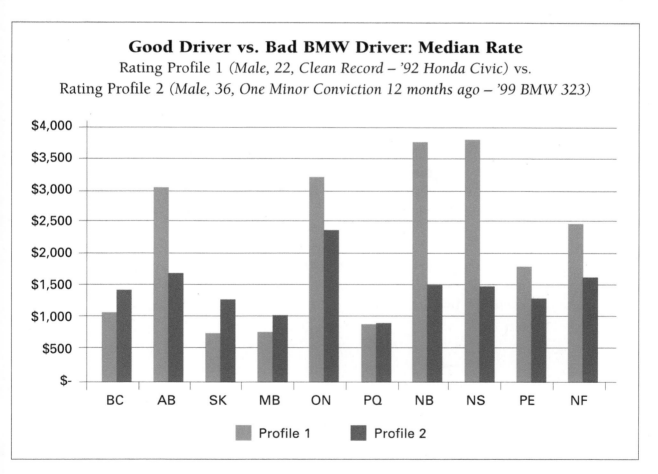

Good Driver vs. Bad BMW Driver: Median Rate

Rating Profile 1 *(Male, 22, Clean Record – '92 Honda Civic)* vs.
Rating Profile 2 *(Male, 36, One Minor Conviction 12 months ago – '99 BMW 323)*

Legend: ■ Profile 1 ■ Profile 2

Source: Data from the Consumers' Association of Canada, "Review of Automobile Insurance Rates: 40 Canadian Cities, 10 Provinces," September 2003.

ACTIVITIES

DIRECTLY STATED IDEAS AND INFORMATION

1. In which provinces does the 22-year-old good driver pay less for car insurance than the older driver with a driving conviction?

2. In which two provinces is the difference between the two rates the greatest?

INDIRECTLY STATED IDEAS AND INFORMATION

3. Based upon the information contained in this selection, explain whether it is better to be a young male driver in Ontario with a clean driving record or an older driver with a conviction.

4. Why do you think some insurance companies charge high rates for younger drivers, even if they have a good driving record?

MAKING CONNECTIONS

5. Why do you think a bar graph was used to present this information? How does this graphical text make statistical information easier to read?

WRITING EXTENSION

Write a news article reporting on the data shown in this graph. Decide what is the most important conclusion you can draw from this graph, and use that to write your headline and your lead.

READING STRATEGY

*Choose four words from the Vocabulary Preview list that you are unsure of. Use the **VOC** strategy that was described on page 95 to learn their meaning. To remember the meaning of the word, you might try one of the following strategies:*

- *connect the word to another similar word*
- *make up a rhyme*
- *form a mental image that expresses the meaning*
- *associate the word with an action*

VOCABULARY PREVIEW

- insight
- smoulders
- induce
- toll
- impasse
- equivalent
- commends
- promote

The Hamilton Spectator   Saturday, June 28, 2003

"I Promise" Drives Safety

❖ by Mike Pettapiece

Gary Direnfeld recalls clearly the day the flash of insight came to him—and almost ran him off the road.

He was driving to Toronto and a flashy car punched into his early-morning commuter's world.

"I was driving down the QEW at 5:30 in the morning and I got cut off by a young guy in a red Camaro. And I wanted to kill him."

Even now, five or six years later, the social work consultant still smoulders at the memory.

Moments later, Direnfeld saw a transport that bore the sign, "How's My Driving?" on its back end. And that's when an idea hatched for a similar sign program for young drivers.

What about a kind of personal contract for driving that young drivers and their parents might join? What if such a thing could induce young people to drive sober and safely—and end the carnage of young deaths on highways?

"That's what twigged me, because I'd phone his [the Camaro driver's] parents."

Enter the I Promise program, now almost two years old, founded and managed by the Dundas resident. His own car has a sign, "Am I Driving Safely?" with a toll-free number. And he and his son, Brennan, have their own contract they swear by.

No calls yet after two years of Brennan driving. And he's cool with the idea, despite what friends may think.

"It doesn't bother me," said the 19-year-old. "My friend asked me [about it] the other day. It's not a huge deal.

"It caused me to drive more safely—to slow down, do small things . . . that make a difference."

Direnfeld knows all about the toll of deaths and brutal injuries involving young drivers and their passengers in car accidents.

He says 6000 young people die annually in North America this way. About 400 000 are injured.

In his social work career, he has seen and worked with brain-injured drivers and passengers. He became very frustrated as the litany of statistics grew right in front of him.

"Somehow, we take teen car crashes as an inevitability. Today, across North America, 16 teens will die and 1100 will be hospitalized. If that were to happen all at once, in one place, can you imagine the outrage?"

If a program could result in young drivers becoming more aware and responsible—maybe even push their parents to be better driving role models—then such a program might have an impact on car crash numbers, health, and insurance costs.

Insurance costs are punitive for a young driver, either with his or her own policy or as part of the family plan. Many young men find their premiums can be $4000 or more, in some cases almost the value of the used car they drive—clean driving record or not.

Such costs are symbolic of a national impasse. Insurance rates for everyone—young and old alike—have gone up, in some cases by more than 50 percent. The rate hikes were so high they pushed the Consumer Price Index to 3 percent in April. Strip out insurance and the core rate was closer to 2 percent.

Ontario's graduated licensing program is good, says Direnfeld, in that it limits young people to the times and highways they can drive. But eventually, he notes, they "fly solo. What then is the response?"

He thinks the answer is I Promise. Parents and their driving teens contract with each other to wear seat belts, to not drink and drive, to avoid in-car distractions, to not speed. Parents must be proper role models in this exercise, he says. . . .

Direnfeld's idea is long on ambition and common sense, but short on pickup by parents, insurance brokers, and insurance companies. He admits candidly that he has fewer than 180 decals out there, in 10 U.S. states and three Canadian provinces.

"So, we've got a lot of breadth but not a lot of depth yet," he says.

Only one insurance carrier, Dominion of Canada General Insurance, backs it and offers an equivalent premium discount to offset the $49 annual cost of the program.

"We believe in it and we support it. We think it's worthwhile," said Mike Ravenscroft, the company's Ontario underwriting manager. "The real key to it is the contract."

Direnfeld parries a question on just how effective a rear-window sign with a phone number can be, especially since the sticker is not overly large or if drivers-by don't have a cell phone.

And what about crank calls? He says there's only been one call, period. And that was from a complimentary caller.

"The issue isn't whether you pick up the number. The issue is whether you have it in back of the car. . . . The goal in this is to promote better driving and we are seeing that happen."

He does have his backers. Down in South Carolina, some people swear by the I Promise program.

One county that picked it up had a decrease in collisions and traffic violations over 2001–2002 compared to a neighbouring county.

In Canada, Transport Minister David Collenette wrote to Direnfeld. In a letter on the www.ipromiseprogram.com Web site, he commends Direnfeld "for your initiative with this program for young drivers."

In Hamilton, the insurance brokers association likes the idea too.

"This [I Promise] is an organization we, as a board, felt would have some merit," said Lorrie Adams, president of the brokers group. "This is a campaign we support."

The Hamilton brokers have helped promote and hand out I Promise literature and have added their logo to materials. Adams says all such public-good ideas often start out slow and small.

"You take Crime Stoppers. At one time, nobody knew who they were, what they did . . . From our standpoint, we wish him success." ∎

ACTIVITIES

DIRECTLY STATED IDEAS AND INFORMATION

1. How has the I Promise program changed Brennan's driving?

2. Explain in your own words why Gary Direnfeld decided to start the I Promise program.

INDIRECTLY STATED IDEAS AND INFORMATION

3. Write a phrase that means the same as the word "drives" in the title.

4. According to this selection, how could the I Promise program lower insurance costs?

MAKING CONNECTIONS

5. Think of your own experiences driving, or those of your friends or acquaintances. Do you think the I Promise program would work to improve people's driving habits? Why or why not?

WRITING EXTENSION

Summarize this reading selection in fewer than 200 words. Make sure you include the main idea of the selection, as well as any details that support the main idea.

READING STRATEGY

DR-TA (Directed Reading-Thinking Activity) is a helpful strategy for longer essays and articles. Look at the title of this piece and predict what you think the selection will be about. Record your prediction in your notebook. After every few paragraphs, stop and revise your prediction based on the new information. Once you have finished reading the selection, write one or two sentences that summarize what it was about.

VOCABULARY PREVIEW

- vibrated
- steep
- veer
- bailing
- tinkering

The Day They Invented the Skateboard

❖ by Bob Schmidt

You may remember the 70s. But I was nine years old in 1961, and I was there the day they invented the skateboard, at least in my neighbourhood.

We took an old metal roller skate and strapped it to a short piece of two-by-four, hopped on top and took off. It was wobblier than hell, moved way too fast, and vibrated on the asphalt enough to jar every bone in your body and loosen every tooth. It was more like getting electrocuted than anything else. We're not talking any hundred dollar baby here. Maybe more like a buck ninety-five. Figure maybe five bucks today for inflation. These were the days when we had hula hoops and Schwinn bicycles. We had Frisbees and yo-yo's and whiffle balls. But we would have traded in any of 'em for our skateboards.

We had a big old hill on Hatherleigh Road in the Stoneleigh community between Baltimore and Towson, Maryland. We all took turns trying it out on that hill. Only a couple of us lived to tell about it. The rest, well, they belong in the skateboard hall of fame. There was me, and Bob Filer, and Hammond Brown, and Barry and Buddy French, Jack Tuttle, and Mike McClellan.

Every one of us fell on our ass and broke at least three bones every year. A leg, an arm, a wrist, a couple of fingers. You couldn't help it. From top to bottom it was a block and a half long. It started out easy, then started curving over until it got a good deal steeper—cars can't get up that hill in the winter after a snow, that's how steep it is.

You had to start down that hill sitting down. Everybody started by sitting on it. There was no way you could go all the way down the first time, even sitting down. You had to get good enough to ride down all the way on your seat, lying flat, trying to keep your feet from hitting the ground. Then starting at the bottom standing up, working your way up a couple of feet at a time, getting your nerve up. It took at least a good two weeks to get it right 'cause you'd have to heal up for a couple of days every time you tried. After a while, there was always somebody walking around with a cast hobbling on crutches and as soon as you saw them you knew it was the Hill.

When you went down the steep section, you got to feeling like you were flying. Then you'd hit a little bump. It wasn't anything you'd even notice on a bike or just walking down, but, man, on a board, look out! If you made it over that bump you'd fly up and just about everybody crashed right there. But once you learned how to twist a little to get past it, well the rest of it was pretty easy. Unless a car was turning into you just as you got down to the bottom. Then you'd have to veer over the curb, bailing out at just the right time so you could run it off onto somebody's lawn.

That hill became the Challenge. You had to beat the Hill. Then you had to beat it three times in a row. And then, well, by then, if you were still alive, you didn't have to do anything.

You were okay. And that's all there was. We didn't jump over curbs. You couldn't anyway, with just a skate underneath. About the only tricks we ever tried were hanging ten off the side or going down on one foot. One guy tried standing on his hands but he fell over and got really messed up by the time he rolled the rest of the way down. A couple of guys tried to be pulled down behind a bike, but they could never do it. Oh, there was a hot dog who tried it every which way, trying to sit on his hands, go down on his belly and stuff, but nobody was impressed.

We were determined to make a faster skateboard you could stay on. We spent months tinkering, smashing down the metal heel at the back of the skate, pulling apart the wheels and mounting them here and there until we got a better balance front to back. We tried every piece of wood we could find. Everybody who was anybody had one of their own they had made. Every one was different. We tried painting them, then we found out the girls liked 'em that way, so we decided that was for sissies and we soaked off the paint and left them plain. But the girls got mad mostly because it was usually one of their skates we were using!

We strapped 'em together. We glued 'em. We nailed 'em. We screwed 'em together. We tried everything. Nothing would hold more than a few times without breaking or coming loose.

Wheels? That was whatever came on a roller skate. Strictly metal. And they only went so fast. Going down the Hill, at some points gravity would be pulling you faster than the wheels could go and half your body would be falling over and that's when you'd get all banged up. Once a wheel was shot, you had to start over. Just about the time you'd get good, you'd have to put another skate on and start all over. And a spare skate wasn't always available. It's not like you could just run up to the store and get one roller skate.

Bearings? What the heck are those? We heard about 'em from somebody's father who was an engineer. But they were kind of sealed into the wheel and you couldn't get at 'em without totally destroying it. But sand and dirt had no problem getting in, and any that did and you were a goner for sure. You'd lock up and go flying at the worst possible time, usually just when you were trying to avoid the handlebars of a bike or a parked car. And we didn't have no truck with trucks. The roller skate was its own truck. You were stuck with it. They never wore out, but they didn't have any cushioning in them either.

Half pipes? What's this wood crap? When we found a half pipe, it wasn't a half pipe at all. It was a giant size concrete sewer pipe, about 8 to 10 feet in diameter. And when you fell onto that, you knew it. They were hard to come by and we hardly ever got to try one. Even then it would only be for a few days or maybe a week during construction.

There was no such thing as a skateboard park. And it was so new, the parents and neighbours didn't even know what to make of it. But they sure knew we were there. Those wheels made a hell of a racket, especially when they needed oil!

And we didn't have any helmets or knee pads, though we probably would have worn 'em if we had 'em. The only padding we had was our own skin and bones.

Yeah, like I tell my son, you can argue about when it was invented, and you can say it ain't so, but I was there the day they invented the skateboard, at least in my neighbourhood.

Even if you're on the right track, you'll get run over if you just sit there.

— *Will Rogers (1879–1935)*
Humorist

ACTIVITIES

DIRECTLY STATED IDEAS AND INFORMATION

1. What was used as the base for the skateboards that the author and his friends created?

2. Why would the bearings on these homemade skateboards sometimes lock up?

INDIRECTLY STATED IDEAS AND INFORMATION

3. Who is the writer talking to? Why does he use casual language such as "a buck ninety-five" and "We strapped 'em together"?

4. Explain why, once a boy beat the hill three times in a row, he was "okay."

MAKING CONNECTIONS

5. According to this selection and your own ideas, explain whether the author and his friends truly "invented" the skateboard.

WRITING EXTENSION

You are a reporter in 1961, writing a human interest story about the boys who "invented" the skateboard. Make sure you include important facts about who, what, where, when, and why.

READING STRATEGY

Before you read the text in this selection, take a look at the pictures. What do you think the red, yellow, and blue arrows show?

VOCABULARY PREVIEW

- performs
- forces
- net
- crucial
- manoeuvre
- pivot
- levelling
- maximum
- unison

Frontside Forces and Fakie Flight
The Physics of Skateboarding Tricks

❖ by Pearl Tesler and Paul Doherty

In the beginning, skateboarding was simple . . .
With nothing more than a two-by-four on roller-skate wheels, the sidewalk surfers of the 30s, 40s, and 50s had a straightforward mission: start at the top of a hill and ride down. The primary goal was just to stay on and avoid collisions; given the humble equipment and rough road conditions, it was no small challenge. Now, thanks in part to improvements in design and materials, skateboarders have a higher calling.

In a blur of flying acrobatics, skaters leap and skid over and onto obstacles, executing flips and turns of ever increasing complexity—all at top speeds. For onlookers and beginners, it can be hard to follow the action, let alone answer the question that springs naturally to mind: How on earth do they do that? While it may seem that modern skateboarders are defying the laws of physics, the truth is that they're just using them to their advantage. Let's take a closer look at one fundamental skateboarding move and the physics principles behind it.

Jumping: The Ollie

Invented in the late 1970s by Alan "Ollie" Gelfand, the ollie has become a skateboarding fundamental, the basis for many other more complicated tricks.

In its simplest form, the ollie is a jumping technique that allows skaters to hop over obstacles and onto curbs, etc. What's so amazing about the ollie is the way the skateboard seems to stick to the skater's feet in midair. Seeing pictures of skaters performing soaring four-foot ollies, many people assume that the board is somehow attached to the skater's feet. It's not. What's even more amazing about the ollie is that to get the skateboard to jump up, the skater pushes down on the board! The secret to this paradoxical manoeuvre is rotation around multiple axes. Let's take a closer look.

1 Just before a skater performs an ollie, there are three forces acting on the skateboard. One of these forces is the weight of the rider, shown here with two **red** arrows. Another is the force of gravity on the board itself, shown with a small **yellow** arrow. Finally, **blue** arrows show the force of the ground pushing up on the skateboard. These three forces balance out to zero. With no net force, the skateboard doesn't accelerate, but rolls along at a constant speed.

Notice that the skater is crouching down. A low centre of mass will be crucial to getting a high jump. (Don't believe it? Stand perfectly straight and try jumping without crouching . . . you didn't get very high, did you?) Now let's follow the changing forces that go into making an ollie.

2 The skater accelerates himself upward by explosively straightening his legs and raising his arms. During the jump, his rear foot exerts a much greater force on the tail of the board than his front foot does on the nose, causing the board to pivot counter-clockwise about the rear wheel.

3 As the tail strikes the ground, the ground exerts a large upward force on the tail. The result of this upward force is that the board bounces up and begins to pivot clockwise, this time around its centre of mass.

4 With the board now completely in the air, the skater slides his front foot forward, using the friction between his foot and the rough surface of the board to drag the board upward even higher.

5 The skater begins to push his front foot down, raising the rear wheels and levelling out the board. Meanwhile, he lifts his rear leg to get it out of the way of the rising tail of the board. If he times this motion perfectly, his rear foot and the rear of the board rise in perfect unison, seemingly "stuck" together.

6 The board is now level at its maximum height. With both feet touching the board, the skater and board begin to fall together under the influence of gravity.

7 Gravity eventually wins out and the skater bends his legs to absorb the impact of the landing.

ACTIVITIES

DIRECTLY STATED IDEAS AND INFORMATION

1. What do the yellow arrows represent in the pictures?

2. What is the purpose of the skater bending his legs as he lands this move?

INDIRECTLY STATED IDEAS AND INFORMATION

3. Explain the purpose of the pictures as they are used in this reading selection.

4. Why do the skater's rear foot and the board seem to be "stuck" together during an ollie?

MAKING CONNECTIONS

5. According to this selection and your own ideas, explain how an understanding of the physics of skateboarding tricks could help a skater perform better.

WRITING EXTENSION

Using the information in this selection, write a bulleted list that gives directions on how to perform an ollie. Include diagrams if you wish.

READING STRATEGY

As you read the facts about Internet usage below, think about your own experiences. Do these statistics reflect trends you have noticed in your life and the lives of your friends?

Internet Statistics

Address: http://www.cyberbullying.ca

Inukshuk.com

www.cyberbullying.ca
"Always On?   Always Aware!"

Home

Examples

What Can Be Done?

Facts and News

Talk the Talk

Related Resources

Contacts

Brought to you
by the creator of

www.bullying.org
"Where You are NOT Alone"

Internet Usage: Facts and News

 = Canadian references

- 99 per cent of Canadian students have used the Internet 🍁
- 48 per cent of Canadian students use it for a least an hour a day 🍁
- Nearly 60 per cent of Canadian students use chat rooms and instant messaging 🍁
- Canadians have the world's highest or near-highest penetration and use of the telephone, cable, TV, computers in the home, and Internet access, especially high-speed Internet access. 🍁
- "By the year 2005, two billion people will be continuously connected to a powerful global network of satellites and fiber optic cables." (–*Innovation Nation*).
- 74 per cent of connected young people use instant messaging several times a week. (–Pew Report)
- 1.2 billion instant messages were sent over the AOL network alone on September 11th, 2001

Address:	http://www.cyberbullying.ca

- By 2005 the annual number of text and visual messages sent over the Internet is expected to reach 1.2 trillion.

- In 2002, cell phone users passed the one billion user mark. This is the fastest 10-year penetration of any product in commercial history.

- China alone is adding five million new cell phone users per month.

- By 2005, most cell phones will come with standard Internet access and a variety of Internet service options.

- A 2002 British survey found that one in four youths aged 11 to 19 have received threats via their computers or cell phones, including death threats.

ACTIVITIES

DIRECTLY STATED IDEAS AND INFORMATION

1. Look at the buttons down the left-hand side of the Web page. Which of these buttons is shown in the selection?

2. How many youths aged 11–19 have received threats via computer or cell phone?

INDIRECTLY STATED IDEAS AND INFORMATION

3. What physical features of Canada do you think might account for the popularity of communication technology such as phones, cable, TV, home computers, and Internet access?

4. Based on what you have read, how would you define "cyberbullying"?

MAKING CONNECTIONS

5. Do you see yourself in any of these statistics? Identify which of the statistics presented here apply to you.

WRITING EXTENSION

Write a letter to an advice columnist from either a victim of cyberbullying, or a bully, asking for help. Then write a reply, in which you give your best advice to help the person.

READING STRATEGY

Before you read this news article, think about school dances, formals, or proms you have been to. Why do you think students would want to attend this sort of function at their high school?

VOCABULARY PREVIEW

◆ sabbatical

◆ emeritus

◆ kindred

◆ chronic

◆ irreversible

San Jose Mercury News   August 30, 2003

A Virtual Prom

❖ by Cynthia Cho

Elle Ward, 16, missed her high school prom and instead spent the evening at home, in bed, because she suffers from chronic fatigue syndrome.

She wrote on an Internet message board the next day: "I want to dance, to laugh, to sing. Proms never come around again."

But Elle's prom did come around again—also on the Internet—thanks to PatchWorx, a Menlo Park-based online community for sick and disabled children.

Several other kids responded to Elle's message, writing that they also had missed their proms or other important events. So on August 13, PatchWorx hosted an "online prom" for approximately 20 teens and their virtual dates—Elle, who lives in a suburb of London, picked *Friends* star Matt Le Blanc—complete with a virtual disk jockey, canapes, and a "terrace" for cooling off.

"We all picked dresses and hair styles and posted them for others to see," Elle said. "It really was one of the best nights ever and made up totally for missing my own real one. It was really fun and one of those rare moments as a sick teen where you forget if only for a minute how ill you are."

In an e-mail to PatchWorx staff from her home in England, Elle's mom, Nora Walsh, wrote that the online prom provided her daughter "with an opportunity in a small way to do some of the things that her healthier peers take for granted."

Giving young people a chance to escape from their lives as sick or disabled is one of the goals of PatchWorx, according to Teresa Middleton, its founder. But the main goal is to give these kids, who range in age from five to 21 and live all over the world, a chance to meet other kids like them.

Middleton founded the non-profit in 1997, when SRI International, where she worked, gave her a six-week paid sabbatical to pursue a project of her choice. Middleton, whose job at SRI involved research into technology and children with disabilities, is now associate director emeritus at SRI, which has donated office space for PatchWorx from its headquarters.

PatchWorx's Web site includes a "Kids Quilt" section where members can post individual profiles (currently there are 102), a "Show-N-Tell" section where members can post art work and writing, and an "Ask Patches" section where members can ask non-health-related questions and share personal stories with Patches, the organization's mascot.

Most of the interaction between members, however, takes place through the message board in adult-moderated chats, where they talk about everything from clothes to first crushes to pop culture— what every teenager is interested in.

"Sometimes the conversation will be centred around things that happen at the Web site, sometimes we talk about things like music and movies, and sometimes everyone will be supporting and listening to one person," said West Hartford, Connecticut, teen Lauren Moynihan, who has participated in two chats.

Many of the young people who join PatchWorx are looking for people who are going through what they are going through. Lori Telson, public relations manager, recalled how excited one PatchWorx member from Pennsylvania became when she found another member from England who had the same illness. "It doesn't matter the location, it's about finding a kindred spirit who understands," Telson said of PatchWorx members.

Many kids who have chronic illnesses or disabilities suffer from isolation and depression, as a result of frequent hospital visits away from friends and family, and from the conditions themselves. "We want to help increase their coping skills for dealing with pain, isolation, and loneliness," Middleton said.

Jesenia Ruiz, 16, recently returned to her home in Miami after undergoing surgery at Lucile Packard Children's Hospital for moya moya, a rare disorder that leads to irreversible blockage of the main blood vessels to the brain as they enter into the skull. Jesenia will have to have another surgery and must take aspirin, to thin the blood, for the rest of her life.

"I have yet to find someone who has it," she said, adding that only one in two million people suffer from the illness. "It would be cool to know someone else."

Middleton said that she often is told by PatchWorx members who participate in chats, "I'm glad to be with people who understand."

Currently, PatchWorx has about 100 active members—kids who chat or post messages on a regular basis—but expects to have 400 by 2005. Using a $426 000 grant from the Department of Commerce in 2002, PatchWorx plans to expand throughout the United States. One way is by forming partnerships with hospitals and clinics; Vanderbilt Children's Hospital in Nashville, Tennessee, and the Ronald McDonald House at Stanford already refer patients to the online community.

"I will never ever understand what it's like to have cancer, even though I work with hundreds of people who have cancer," said Janet Cross, Child Life Director at Vanderbilt Children's Hospital. "The kids become unique by having an illness or disability and the opportunity to share their feelings and experiences with someone else who understands is very important." ■

A life is not important except in its impact on the lives of others.

— *Jackie Robinson (1919–1972)*
Baseball Hall of Famer

ACTIVITIES

DIRECTLY STATED IDEAS AND INFORMATION

1. Why were the students in this selection unable to attend their high school proms?

2. Describe the two main goals of PatchWorx.

INDIRECTLY STATED IDEAS AND INFORMATION

3. Explain how attending an online prom could help sick teens feel better.

4. How will forming partnerships with hospitals and clinics help PatchWorx expand?

MAKING CONNECTIONS

5. Based on your own experience and what you have read, explain how the Internet community is different from, and similar to, a traditional community, such as a neighbourhood or town.

WRITING EXTENSION

Research on the Internet to find out about chronic fatigue syndrome. Then write a one-page information sheet on the disease. Use subheadings such as "Symptoms" and "Treatment" to break up the text. You may also want to use bullets or other text features to present parts of the information.

READING STRATEGY

*This story is divided into sections of text. Read the first section, down to the words, "I start remembering again." What can you **predict** from this introduction? Continue to predict and **reflect** as you move through each section of the story.*

Starr

❖ by Angela Johnson

I remembered her today because I went downtown and looked for new shoes. My friend May came with me to buy herself a black sweatshirt. It's all she wears. I don't think I've ever seen her in anything else.

We took the express bus downtown after school let out. May stuck her feet on the seat in front of her.

"Every time I get on this bus it's so full of people I can't get off at my stop."

She pulled the cord one stop short of where we were going, for the fun of it, hoping the bus would empty. The last person to get off at that stop wore her hair in a bun.

That's when the remembering started.

You can go all day and put all the things that hurt you away in your head. You never have to talk about them, think about them, or feel them. I've been doing it for so long and am so good at it. . . .

Sometimes when I'm at the arcade and I feel like I am totally gone from my body, it will happen. Or I could be at the park under a tree looking up at the sky and *bam!*

I start remembering again.

Starr used to take me to Venice Beach on the hot afternoons when it probably would have made more sense to stay at home under some shade, sucking up orange bubble-gum ices and pineapple pizza.

I'd fought with Jimmy that fourteen was too old for a baby-sitter, but he'd just straightened his tie and shook his head. I like my dad, Jimmy, even though what he says usually goes; even if I hate it. He doesn't put his foot down much, except the time I wanted to paint my room black and buy snakes.

I guess since it's been just me and Jimmy, he's used to me and my moods and doesn't even look surprised any more. But he wasn't backing down about a sitter.

Starr showed up on a mountain bike painted Day-Glo at our little house off Sunset. Jimmy took one look at her and closed the door in her face. He'd interviewed her on the phone, by fax and e-mail, but never in person. He couldn't believe the shaved-head and pierced-lip girl in the COOK THE RICH SLOWLY T-shirt was the Ph.D. in psychology he'd spent an entire lunch break interviewing.

In the end, he opened the door again.

Starr stepped in smiling and sat down cross-legged in front of Jimmy and listened to Basic Baby-sitter 411. She kept smiling, and in the end Jimmy and her were talking about seventies funk bands, and that gave me a headache, but it kept Starr in the house.

By the time Jimmy backed down the drive, Starr and I were eating peanut butter off of spoons and listening to some reggae she had recorded at some club off the Strip.

May says that I wouldn't be having as bad a time as I'm having if I had just accepted Starr as a sitter and not some kind of mother-friend. May thinks that you shouldn't get too close to anybody. She has three stepfathers, two stepmothers, five half brothers, three half sisters, fifteen stepbrothers and sisters, and enough grandparents that she opens gifts all Christmas morning. I figure she doesn't have to make friends. She has relatives.

May could be right. But after a few days being with Starr, it was too late.

I have some of Starr's bandannas. She used to wear them over her nose and mouth when she rode her bike. She said that the smog got to her. She had tons of them, all different colours and sizes. She never picked them to match what she was wearing. She picked them by how she felt when she got up and what she remembered about the day she bought them.

(Remembering. She got into it first.)

Once we were at an open café on the beach when Starr jumped over the wall and walked up to a man in a wool poncho reading tarot cards. I watched her as I drank my iced tea. She sat smacking on an avocado sandwich in a folding chair, nodding her head.

The man took her hand and started nodding back. He pointed out to the ocean, and, just then, Starr looked over at me and waved. I waved but felt so sad and didn't know why.

After that we'd run through the water in our clothes and got so soaked we stuck to the bus seats all the way home.

Last summer I saw Starr more than Jimmy. When I woke up in the morning, she was there. When I went to sleep at night, she was there.

Jimmy trusted her so much he just sort of started living in his office—which is what he would have done all the time if it hadn't been for me. I guess it was like May said: Starr became my mother-friend. She was what I needed, and I guess I was what she needed, too.

I knew it the day we went to visit her mama in the desert.

I got up early and Starr was standing in the kitchen fixing chocolate-chip pancakes. She'd started sleeping in the spare room and pretty much lived in our house by then. It worked for Jimmy—who was already gone for the day.

"You up already, Nic?"

I stubbed my toe on the old Formica table I'd talked Jimmy into buying at a used-furniture store off Van Nuys.

"Sort of, I guess." I rubbed my toe as I started to eat the pancakes Starr had put in front of me. She sat down across from me, sipping coffee and staring.

She said, "Would you miss me if I went away? I don't mean right now . . ."

I thought about it for a while, not because I didn't know the answer. I was just thinking of a way to put it. I mean I'm not like that, touchy-feely and always being honest about stuff like that. Jimmy raised me, for God's sake.

I chewed my pancakes until they had dissolved.

"I don't have to miss you," I said. "You're here."

"Yeah, I know that, but people do go. They go on and sometimes they even go back. I just wanted to know if you'd have a hard time with the going."

"I really don't know 'cause I haven't had too many people go away from me, except my mom, and I don't even remember her. I guess that doesn't count. I don't know—"

Starr started laughing and drank more coffee.

"It's okay. It's no big deal. I just wondered about it."

Starr played with her lip ring and got up from the table. She winked at me and started washing up the dishes. Two hours later we were barrelling towards the desert, and I'd forgotten what we'd talked about.

May told me I don't pay enough attention to things. She said I'm not the kind of person who always has toilet paper trailing behind me, but I don't notice if somebody else does.

I loved the desert and Starr's parents. They were old hippies who made ceramics and had posters of Malcolm X and Margaret Sanger on their walls, and hadn't touched meat in thirty years.

They loved Starr and never said one thing about the way she looked. She was thirty-two and a baby-sitter. I knew from the way my friends' parents talked about their kids, Starr would have had a bad time in their homes.

All Starr's parents did was hug her a lot, feed me too many organic vegetables, and talk about the sixties. They showed me pictures of Starr when they lived on a commune, and pictures of them at some concert. They both had big Afros and were hugging.

Starr looked at them and smiled.

I got that sad feeling and couldn't shake it. I remember thinking I was probably just missing Jimmy.

On the way back to L.A. I fell asleep lying across Starr. I fell asleep to her singing a song I remembered my grandmama singing to me. It was just a song, but it made me feel warm and safe. The bus drove into the sunset.

By the end of the summer I'd grown two inches and was just about sick of pineapples. Jimmy got a promotion, and May got her braces off and started hanging out with some guy who wanted to be a rapper. Every time you saw him he had a Snapple in his hand. Starr told May this guy was as hyper as he was because of all the sugar.

May says I always take too long to finish a story, and maybe that's true. It's okay. I don't think people talk all that much to each other anymore. I know they talk *at* each other—all you have to do is watch those talk shows. Starr wouldn't let me watch them. She said that it was porno for the stupid and bored.

Anyway, summer was almost over and Jimmy was starting to be home more. I guess that's what he got out of the promotion. Starr had started to spend most of the day looking out the window at the road. Sometimes she'd count the number of Porsches that went by, other days it was Mercedes or Jeeps.

Some days she'd just look out the window and keep repeating every half hour or so that summer was gone. That would depress me and make me feel lonely. I didn't know why.

Jimmy says even though he knew, maybe he should have been on it a little more.

The last morning Starr pulled up to the door on her mountain bike, she was wearing hair. Simple hair. Not purple, spiked, or any style I'd have expected from Starr. She wore a wig pinned up in a bun. The lip ring was gone, and she was wearing what Jimmy calls adult clothes. She walked in the door and held me. Jimmy took one look at her and left.

It's funny when you see people with bald heads. Most of us think fashion. I guess at fourteen you shouldn't be thinking of cancer and dying. Dying and cancer.

She'd told Jimmy on the phone the first time she'd talked to him that she was sick. She told him she needed to be needed.

Jimmy cries when he tells me he hadn't wanted to be needed so much by me.

Starr and me rode the bus to the beach and walked along the water until both our stomachs started growling. We sucked down bean and chicken burritos till we couldn't move. Then we watched the show go by.

I looked at Starr in her adult clothes and wig.

"What did the tarot reader tell you in June?"

Starr sipped her iced tea and grinned at a man on in-lines with a monkey on his head. She loved Venice Beach.

"He told me I'd recently had a life-altering experience."

Then she pulled off her wig at the table and threw it to a waiter.

Jimmy bought me this bike for my fifteenth birthday, and two days later I painted it Day-Glo orange. He doesn't really like orange bubble-gum ices, but he'll choke one down for me. He says I've really grown up in the last year and it looks like I won't be needing a baby-sitter this summer.

I helped Jimmy straighten his tie. Then I shook my head slowly, even though I knew he was right.

ACTIVITIES

DIRECTLY STATED IDEAS AND INFORMATION

1. On what issues does Jimmy put his foot down?

2. How does Starr's appearance surprise Jimmy?

INDIRECTLY STATED IDEAS AND INFORMATION

3. At the end of the story, Starr reveals that the tarot card reader told her she had "recently had a life-altering experience." What experience do you think she is referring to?

4. In your opinion, how has the narrator changed by the end of the story? Give evidence from the text to support your ideas.

MAKING CONNECTIONS

5. What do you think of May's idea that "you shouldn't get too close to anybody"? Is this a reasonable reaction to the loss of a loved one?

WRITING EXTENSION

Think of someone who has had a significant impact on your life. It could be a family member, or someone outside the family. Write a one-page profile of this person that sums up the influence he or she had on your life. Include an introduction that states how the subject influenced you, and a conclusion that summarizes your feelings towards him or her.

Reflecting on Your Learning

This section will give you a chance to think back over the past unit, reflect upon what you have learned, and apply it to your future learning.

READING SKILLS

1. What is one thing you can do when you come to a word you are unfamiliar with in a selection?

2. Describe one way your reading skills have improved after completing this unit.

WRITING / COMMUNICATION SKILLS

3. Make a list of the different types of writing you did in this unit. In a small group, brainstorm a list of text and stylistic features for each type of writing. Then fill in the chart below on your own.

Type of Writing	Features I Included	Features I Didn't Include

Could any of your pieces be improved if you revised them to include the features in the third column?

4. Find evidence in your schoolwork or your everyday life that your communication skills (writing, speaking, or listening) have improved since you began this course.

LEARNING SKILLS

5. Name one reading, writing, or communicating skill you used in this unit that could help you in another course you are taking. Be specific.

LOOKING AHEAD

6. Based on all of the information above, set two learning goals for yourself for the next few weeks. What strategies do you plan on using to accomplish these goals?

Making a Difference

What are your goals? What do you hope to achieve in your lifetime? In this unit, you'll explore how you and others can make a difference—to yourself, to your fellow human beings, and to the planet. Many of the selections in this unit profile individuals who have reached out to help others, either in their own communities or globally. Throughout the unit, you will see that words and images can be a powerful source for positive change.

READING STRATEGY

This strategy is called **Save the Last Word for Me**. *Here is how it works:*

1. *Read the selection. While you are reading, search for three statements that stand out for you for some reason. Perhaps these statements made you think, made you angry, or reminded you of something else.*
2. *Write each statement on an index card or a strip of paper. On the back, write down your reaction to the statement.*
3. *Work with a group to share your statements. One group member passes around an index card. Moving around the group, each member has the opportunity to react to the statement. The group member who introduced it gets the "last word." The next group member passes around an index card, and the process continues.*
4. *As a group, decide upon the two most significant things you have learned.*

VOCABULARY PREVIEW

- ◆ tempting
- ◆ responsible
- ◆ examine
- ◆ consciously
- ◆ purposefully
- ◆ relentless

Ending the Blame Game

❖ by Roberta Beecroft

"Hey! I'm not happy and it's your fault! So, change!" We do some crazy things when we don't like the way our life is going. Too often we blame someone else.

"If only you treated me as nicely as Jason treats Allison."

"I wish my parents were more generous and understanding."

"I have such a lousy Chemistry teacher!"

"My friends are so boring and self-centred. They make my life miserable."

Blame! Blame! Blame!

It's tempting to sing this self-pitying song, but the truth is, if you don't like your life, you are responsible for doing something about it. No one else is responsible for your happiness. No one else knows exactly how you feel or what you need. No one can read your mind magically and grant your every wish. You are the only one with the right and the opportunity to examine your life, and if you want it to be different, you can change what you're doing. You can take clear, definite steps to act on your own behalf. You can choose an active approach to situations instead of simply reacting to someone else's behaviour.

This means asking . . . "*What do I need? What do I want to do? What am I willing to do?*" instead of focusing only on others' demands. For example, it means deciding how you want to spend your evening instead of groaning, "*Oh no! Lisa's so depressed she'll expect me to spend the whole night listening to her on the phone!*" We teach other people how we're willing to be treated. If we don't respect our own needs and limits, no one else will either.

Right about now I can hear you working up your "yeah, but" argument . . . "*Yeah, but you don't know my principal!*" . . . "*Yeah, but you don't have to live with my brother!*" . . . "*Yeah, but you don't have to watch your ex-sweetheart making out with her latest, two lockers away: you wouldn't like it either and you'd feel bad and put-down, too.*"

In difficult situations, don't give away your power to decide how you feel about yourself. Choose—thoughtfully, consciously choose—your response to the situations in your life. Choose how you want to think and act. Other people can't **make** you unhappy or angry. Other people behave as they do and then it's up to you to decide how you will respond. For example: your friends went out to lunch without you. You feel angry, left out, insecure. How are you going to act in this situation? You could blame your friends . . . "*They're so thoughtless and inconsiderate: who needs them anyway?*" or you could tell your friends how you feel, listen to their explanation, and let them know you'd like to be included next time.

When you take responsibility for your actions, when you act purposefully, you're grasping hold of your own life, shaping it according to your beliefs, your values, and feelings. Make choices instead of waiting for others to have an impact on you. It's up to you. You can choose to be happy, to make friends, to build an interesting life. When you blame others for what is or isn't happening in your life, you get stuck and stop growing and learning.

One of the most important "laws of human nature" is that you can never, ever change another person by your direct action. The **only** person you have the right and power to change is yourself. Once you change, the other person then has something different to respond to and change is possible. If you want change in your life, begin with yourself . . . add love, respect, gentleness, and a relentless belief in your power to take action.

Goodbye blame! Hello, self-esteem!

Everyone is necessarily the hero
of his own life story.

— *John Barth (b. 1930)*
Writer

ACTIVITIES

DIRECTLY STATED IDEAS AND INFORMATION

1. According to this selection, if you don't like your life, who should you get to change it?

2. According to this selection, what is one of the most important laws of human nature?

INDIRECTLY STATED IDEAS AND INFORMATION

3. What is the purpose of the phrases that are written in italics throughout this selection?

4. Look at the last sentence in this selection. Explain how people's self-esteem will increase if they stop blaming others for the way their life is going.

MAKING CONNECTIONS

5. In this selection, the author describes a situation where someone gets left out of a group lunch. Think about a situation in which you felt left out, and describe how you reacted to it. Looking back, could you have dealt with it better?

WRITING EXTENSION

Write a summary of this article. Make sure you begin with a clear main idea and provide details to support that idea. Remember that a summary should include only the opinions and information contained in the original selection.

READING STRATEGY
This song lyric is written with line breaks like a poem. Read the text aloud. As you are reading, don't pause at the end of each line, but rather where you think it makes sense.

VOCABULARY PREVIEW

- frustrations
- stilted
- defence
- sacrifice
- yield

The Living Years

❖ by Mike Rutherford and B.A. Robertson

Every generation
Blames the one before
And all of their frustrations
Come beating on your door

I know that I'm a prisoner
To all my father held so dear
I know that I'm a hostage
To all his hopes and fears
I just wish I could have told him in the living years

Crumpled bits of paper
Filled with imperfect thought
Stilted conversations
I'm afraid that's all we've got

You say you just don't see it
He says it's perfect sense
You just can't get agreement
In this present tense
We all talk a different language
Talking in defence

Say it loud, say it clear
You can listen as well as you hear
It's too late when we die
To admit we don't see eye to eye

So we open up a quarrel
Between the present and the past
We only sacrifice the future
It's the bitterness that lasts

So don't yield to the fortunes
You sometimes see as fate
It may have a new perspective
On a different day
And if you don't give up, and don't give in
You may just be O.K.

Say it loud, say it clear
You can listen as well as you hear
It's too late when we die
To admit we don't see eye to eye

I wasn't there that morning
When my father passed away
I didn't get to tell him
All the things I had to say

I think I caught his spirit
Later that same year
I'm sure I heard his echo
In my baby's newborn tears
I just wish I could have told him in the living years

Say it loud, say it clear
You can listen as well as you hear
It's too late when we die
To admit we don't see eye to eye

ACTIVITIES

DIRECTLY STATED IDEAS AND INFORMATION

1. Why was the narrator upset that he wasn't there when his father passed away?

2. What event followed the death of the narrator's father that allowed him to "catch his [father's] spirit"?

INDIRECTLY STATED IDEAS AND INFORMATION

3. Explain what is meant in the second stanza by the phrase "I know that I'm a prisoner / To all my father held so dear."

4. Why do you think the songwriters wrote this song?

MAKING CONNECTIONS

5. Explain whether you think "The Living Years" is a good title for this song.

WRITING EXTENSION

In a well-written opinion piece, explain whether you believe it's true that "every generation blames the one before." Make sure you have a clear main idea and that you support your opinion with at least three supporting details.

READING STRATEGY
*When you read through the poem, pause when you see
punctuation, rather than at the end of each line.*

Johnnie's Poem

❖ by Alden Nowlan

Look! I've written a poem!
Johnnie says
and hands it to me

         and it's about

         his grandfather dying

         last summer, and me

         in the hospital

and I want to cry,
don't you see, because it doesn't matter
if it's not very good:

         what matters most is he knows

and it was me, his father, who told him

         you write poems about what

         you feel deepest and hardest.

ACTIVITIES

DIRECTLY STATED IDEAS AND INFORMATION

1. According to the narrator, what do you write poems about?

2. What personal experience did Johnnie write a poem about?

INDIRECTLY STATED IDEAS AND INFORMATION

3. What personal experience caused *the author* to write his poem?

4. Why is the narrator so touched by his son's poem?

MAKING CONNECTIONS

5. "You write poems about what you feel deepest and hardest." List five subjects people write poems [and songs] about.

WRITING EXTENSION

What do you think Johnnie's poem was like? Write your own version of Johnnie's poem.

READING STRATEGY

Our focus can be distracted when we view a graphic text that includes words. Try turning your page upside down, or looking at the image backwards, in order to get a better sense of the shape and the design elements.

Steps to a Better Life

ACTIVITIES

DIRECTLY STATED IDEAS AND INFORMATION

1. Describe the main visual elements in this graphic text.

2. What will climbing the steps lead you to?

INDIRECTLY STATED IDEAS AND INFORMATION

3. What is meant by "know yourself" and why is it on the very first step?

4. How has the designer used light and dark in the graphic? How does the design of this graphic add to the meaning?

MAKING CONNECTIONS

5. Why did the author/illustrator use the image of a set of ascending steps? What other images would fit this idea?

WRITING EXTENSION

Write your own nine-step plan for your immediate future, which you think will lead you to a better life.

READING STRATEGY

*Use the **SCAN** cues to preview the selection:*
***S**urvey headings. Turn them into questions.*
***C**apture (scan) the captions and visuals*
***A**ttack boldface or italicized words. Are they singled out as key terms or for emphasis?*
***N**ote and read the questions at the end.*

*While reading the selection, use the three **RUN** cues:*
***R**ead. Slow down for harder sections.*
***U**se word identification skills for difficult words. Sound them out, look for context clues, or break them into parts.*
***N**otice parts you don't understand. Decide whether to reread them now or mark them and go back later.*

VOCABULARY PREVIEW

- benefiting
- informed
- immune
- consequences
- endurance
- exposed

The Scoop

Address:	http://www.hc-sc.gc.ca/

Health Canada   Santé Canada   **Canada**

Contact Us	Help	Search
The Scoop	Quit 4 Life	The Industry	Study It!

HOME
THE SCOOP
Cigarettes Inside Out >
Warning: Pack Pics >
Got Skillz? >
Real Cost >
"It will never > happen to me"
Second-hand Smoke >

The Scoop

What's the deal with smoking?

By giving you the facts about what smoking means to your body, your environment and who's actually benefiting from the sale of tobacco products we hope you'll make an informed decision about sticking that cigarette in your mouth and lighting up.

Address: http://www.hc-sc.gc.ca/

HOME
THE SCOOP
Cigarettes Inside Out >
Warning: Pack Pics >
Got Skillz? >
Real Cost >
"It will never >
happen to me"
Second-hand Smoke >

Speak Out!
Take part in our 2nd
hand smoke poll

CHECK IT OUT

- Tobacco smoke is made up mainly of tar (which builds up in your lungs), nicotine and carbon monoxide. It also contains other **poisonous substances** like cyanide, formaldehyde and ammonia.

- Smokeless tobacco (chewing tobacco, snuff) is also very dangerous to health. Smokeless tobacco users are more likely to develop cancer of the mouth, lip, tongue, gums, and throat. You are also more likely to develop dental problems such as cavities, tooth loss and gum disease.

- The nicotine in tobacco is one of the most addictive substances known. About eight out of every ten people who try smoking get hooked.

- Tobacco use causes many different kinds of cancer—and not just lung cancer. Think mouth, throat, pancreas, bladder, kidney and cervix. Then there's respiratory and heart disease.

- Young women who smoke and are taking birth control pills increase their chances for serious heart disease, stroke and high blood pressure.

- **Second-hand smoke** can cause lung cancer among non-smokers.

- A Canadian dies every 12 minutes of a tobacco related disease.

- Tobacco smoke kills over 45,000 people in Canada each year. That's more than the total of all murders, alcohol-related deaths, car accidents and suicides.

Estimated Deaths In Canada, 1996

■ Murders — 510

■ Alcohol — 1,500

■ Car Accidents — 2,500

■ Suicides — 3,500

■ Tobacco — 45,000

WARNING
EACH YEAR, THE EQUIVALENT
OF A SMALL CITY DIES
FROM TOBACCO USE

It's Never Going to Happen to Me

Yeah, right. When we're young and strong, it's so easy to think that cancer and heart disease only happen to other people. Much older people. You're immune, right? Wrong.

Here's a sobering way to look at the situation:

- Among young people, the short-term health consequences of smoking include respiratory effects—cough and increased frequency and severity of illnesses like asthma, chest colds and bronchitis—as well as addiction to nicotine.

- In adults, cigarette smoking causes heart disease and stroke. Early signs of these diseases can be found in adolescents who smoke.

Address: http://www.hc-sc.gc.ca/

HOME

THE SCOOP

Cigarettes Inside Out >

Warning: Pack Pics >

Got Skillz? >

Real Cost >

"It will never happen > to me" >

Second-hand Smoke >

Speak Out!
Take part in our 2nd hand smoke poll

CHECK IT OUT

- The younger people start smoking, the more likely they are to become strongly addicted to nicotine.

- Most young people who smoke regularly continue to smoke throughout adulthood.

- Smoking reduces the rate of lung growth and it can hamper the level of maximum lung function.

- According to the US Center for Disease Control, high school seniors who are regular smokers and began smoking by grade nine are more than twice as likely as their non-smoking peers to report poorer overall health, cough with phlegm or blood, shortness of breath when not exercising, and wheezing or gasping.

- Smoking at an early age increases the risk of lung cancer.

Did You Know . . .

Good news or bad, we've got facts and figures to help you make up your mind about smoking.

The good . . .

- The latest Canadian statistics show that fewer teenagers aged 15-19 are smoking. In 2001, only 22.5% of teens aged 15-19 smoked; that's down from 28% in 1999!

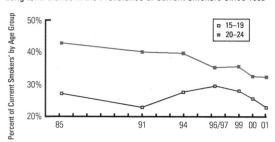

Long term Trends in the Prevalence of Current Smokers Since 1985

- Teen smokers lead the way when it comes to quitting. In fact 25% of teen smokers were actively trying to quit in 2000.

The bad . . .

- Teen girls start smoking earlier than boys and more girls 15 to 19 years old smoke (24% vs 21% in 2001)

- In 2001, an estimated 800,000 kids under 12 were regularly exposed to second-hand smoke in the home from cigarettes, cigars or pipes.

- One tree is lost for every 300 cigarettes manufactured.

Address: http://www.hc-sc.gc.ca/

And the ugly.

- Approximately half of all smokers die from a smoking-related illness—cancer, heart disease and other ailments.

- Canadian teenagers smoke more than 1.6 billion cigarettes each year—resulting in retail sales worth more than $330 million. Just think about what else could be done with that money.

- More than 1,000 non-smokers will die this year in Canada due to tobacco use—over 300 lung cancer deaths and at least 700 deaths from coronary heart disease will be caused by second-hand smoke.

ACTIVITIES

DIRECTLY STATED IDEAS AND INFORMATION

1. In the 15- to 19-year-old age range, is smoking more popular with girls or boys?

2. Why is it dangerous to smoke while taking birth control pills?

INDIRECTLY STATED IDEAS AND INFORMATION

3. What two parts of this Web page are like the table of contents in a book?

4. According to the latest Canadian statistics, what is happening to the number of teenagers aged 15 to 19 who smoke? Explain why you think this trend is taking place.

MAKING CONNECTIONS

5. Given the health and financial effects of smoking, explain why you believe people begin smoking at all.

WRITING EXTENSION

Write an information paragraph using facts from the bulleted lists in this selection. Use at least five facts that focus on one aspect of the topic.

READING STRATEGY

This selection contains a chart. Run your eyes over the headings on the chart to get a sense of what it contains.

VOCABULARY PREVIEW

◆ average

◆ perspective

Smoking: Not a Cheap Thrill

Before you take that first puff, what's it going to cost you? Let's say you start smoking at age 13 (some do) and smoke an average of 25 cigarettes every day. By the time you turn 30, you will have spent about $37 000 on cigarettes (at $6 a pack). Just think about what you could have done with that money. Buy a car. Spend a summer in Europe. Pay for university. Puts it in perspective doesn't it?

Do the math . . .

If you smoke 11 cigarettes a day and spend $5.95 on a pack of 25 cigarettes, the chart below shows what you could have bought over a time period of 5 years.

Time	Cost	Alternative
1 day	$2.62	Snacks
3 days	$7.85	Lunch
5 days	$13.09	Movie ticket
1 week	$18.33	X-L Pizza
2 weeks	$36.65	Tank of gas
3 weeks	$54.98	Bus pass
1 month	$78.54	Leather basketball
2 months	$157.08	MP3 player
3 months	$235.62	Leather jacket
6 months	$476.48	Snowboard
1 year	$955.57	Stereo system
3 years	$2866.71	Computer
5 years	$4777.85	A really nice vacation

THE FAR SIDE **BY GARY LARSON**

The Far Side® by Gary Larson © 1982 FarWorks, Inc. All Rights Reserved. Used with permission.

© 1982 FarWorks, Inc. All Rights Reserved/Dist. by Creators Syndicate

The real reason dinosaurs became extinct

ACTIVITIES

DIRECTLY STATED IDEAS AND INFORMATION

1. According to the cartoon, what is the "real" reason dinosaurs became extinct?

2. How many months would a person have to stop smoking in order to be able to buy a snowboard?

INDIRECTLY STATED IDEAS AND INFORMATION

3. The cartoon and the chart use different approaches to convince the reader not to smoke. Explain the strategy used in each case.

4. Explain what age group this selection is targeting and how you know that.

MAKING CONNECTIONS

5. Do you believe this selection will be effective in getting people to stop smoking? Support your belief with evidence.

WRITING EXTENSION

Pretend that the cartoon is a newspaper picture and the caption "The real reason dinosaurs became extinct" is the headline. Write a newspaper article to go with the picture. You will need to make up the details in the newspaper article.

READING STRATEGY

Scan this text to find out why the information has been placed on a map of the world.

Costs of Smoking

VOCABULARY PREVIEW

◆ benefits
◆ revenues
◆ social welfare
◆ foreign exchange
◆ deforestation
◆ premiums
◆ touting

The tobacco industry uses economic arguments to persuade governments, the media, and the general population that smoking benefits the economy. It claims that if tobacco control measures are introduced, tax revenues will fall, jobs will be lost, and there will be great hardship to the economy.

But the industry greatly exaggerates the economic losses, if any, which tobacco control measures will cause and they never mention the economic costs which tobacco inflicts upon every country.

Tobacco's cost to governments, to employers, and to the environment includes social, welfare, and health care spending; loss of foreign exchange in importing cigarettes; loss of land that could grow food; costs of fires and damage to buildings caused by careless smoking; environmental costs ranging from deforestation to collection of smokers' litter; absenteeism, decreased productivity, higher numbers of accidents, and higher insurance premiums.

$ Canada 1.6 billion

$ USA 76 billion

$ Health-care costs

Health care costs (US$) attributable to tobacco, *2002* or latest available estimates, selected countries

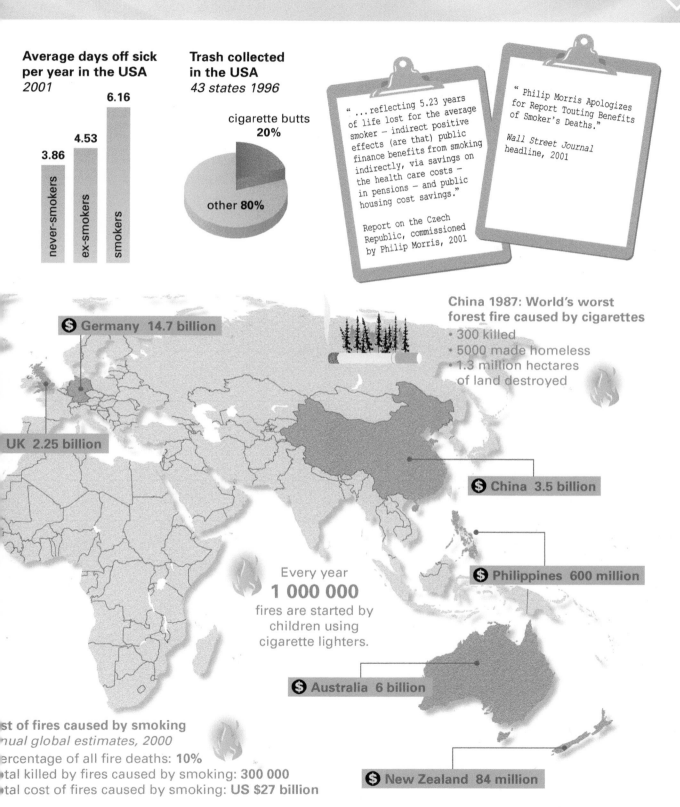

Average days off sick per year in the USA
2001

- never-smokers 3.86
- ex-smokers 4.53
- smokers 6.16

Trash collected in the USA
43 states 1996

- cigarette butts **20%**
- other **80%**

" ...reflecting 5.23 years of life lost for the average smoker – indirect positive effects (are that) public finance benefits from smoking indirectly, via savings on the health care costs – in pensions – and public housing cost savings."

Report on the Czech Republic, commissioned by Philip Morris, 2001

" Philip Morris Apologizes for Report Touting Benefits of Smoker's Deaths."

Wall Street Journal headline, 2001

China 1987: World's worst forest fire caused by cigarettes
- 300 killed
- 5000 made homeless
- 1.3 million hectares of land destroyed

$ Germany 14.7 billion

UK 2.25 billion

$ China 3.5 billion

$ Philippines 600 million

Every year
1 000 000
fires are started by children using cigarette lighters.

$ Australia 6 billion

$ New Zealand 84 million

st of fires caused by smoking
nual global estimates, 2000
- ercentage of all fire deaths: **10%**
- tal killed by fires caused by smoking: **300 000**
- tal cost of fires caused by smoking: **US $27 billion**

ACTIVITIES

DIRECTLY STATED IDEAS AND INFORMATION

1. Use information from the bar graph to compare the average days off sick of a smoker and a non-smoker.

2. Create a chart to show the health-care costs of smoking. List the countries mentioned and the amount that each country spends annually on health care.

3. As well as health-care costs, what other economic costs are mentioned in the graphic?

INDIRECTLY STATED IDEAS AND INFORMATION

4. How does the use of colour add to the impact of this graphic text?

5. What is the problem with the tobacco industry's use of economic arguments to support smoking?

MAKING CONNECTIONS

6. Choose one fact from this graphic that impressed or surprised you the most, and explain why.

WRITING EXTENSION

Write a one-page letter to the Philip Morris Company, responding to their apology. Use a formal tone in your writing, and present your opinion in proper letter form.

READING STRATEGY

This excerpt from a history textbook contains several features and visuals that are set off from the text. Before you read, identify each of these features and visuals and what each contains. This will help you to answer the Making Connections question.

VOCABULARY PREVIEW

- seized
- recalled
- referred
- opposed
- decipher
- estimated
- successful
- abolitionists

The Underground Railroad

❖ by J. Bradley Cruxton and W. Douglas Wilson

"When my feet first touched the Canada shore I threw myself on the ground, rolled around in the sand, seized handfuls of it and kissed it and danced around, till, in the eyes of several who were present, I passed for a madman." This is how Josiah Henson recalled his arrival to freedom in Canada in 1830.

Josiah Henson was one of the former Black slaves* who came to Canada by way of the Underground Railroad. In spite of its name, the Underground Railroad was not a real railroad. The term referred to a network of people and safe houses that helped runaway slaves. The Underground Railroad provided an escape route from the United States to Canada.

Governor Simcoe [of Upper Canada] was a firm opponent of slavery. He had introduced an anti-slavery bill in the first Legislative Assembly in 1792. It did not outlaw slavery,

FIGHTING FOR FREEDOM

A number of Black Canadians were involved in the efforts to abolish slavery in the United States and to help slaves when they arrived in Canada:

- Mary Ann Shadd, a freeborn woman of colour, was a well-known teacher, writer, lawyer, and newspaper publisher
- Ruffin Abbott, the first Black doctor born in Canada
- Reverend Samuel Ringgold Ward, publisher of a newspaper dealing with the problems encountered by refugee Blacks
- Henry Bibb, who published a Windsor, Ontario, newspaper to help newly escaped slaves

but it did state that no new slaves could be imported to Upper Canada and that no one

* Currently, the phrase "enslaved people" is often used in place of the term "slaves" and is considered more respectful. Students and teachers may wish to discuss how these two terms are different and why one might be preferred over the other.

was to be enslaved for any reason. Slavery was abolished throughout the British Empire by 1834 but continued for a number of years in other parts of the world.

After the War of 1812, Canada gained the reputation of being a safe place for runaway slaves from America. American soldiers returning from the war to their homes in the South talked about Upper Canada. They told of the Canadian government's willingness to defend the rights of Black people. Gradually, by word of mouth among slaves, Canada became known as the "land of promise."

In their efforts to escape, some of the slaves discovered that they could count on the help of a number of people in the northern states. These were often religious people who opposed slavery. They were called abolitionists because they wanted to abolish slavery. They were willing to take risks to help runaway slaves get to the safety of Canada.

There was always a need for secrecy because there were bounty hunters looking for runaway slaves. The Fugitive Slave Law in the United States had given owners the right to chase and capture their slaves in any state. Bounty hunters were given rewards by slave owners when they captured and returned the runaways.

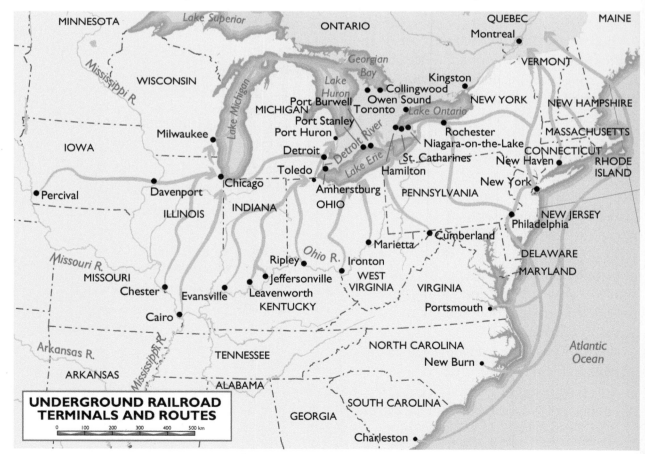

UNDERGROUND RAILROAD TERMINALS AND ROUTES

To hide and disguise their efforts, the abolitionists used railway terms. The people who led the slaves on foot or horseback or transported them by wagon, barge, or steamer became known as "conductors." The runaways, often hidden in crates, were called "cargo" or "passengers." Hiding places such as barns, cellars, attics, and church towers were called "stations." The people who helped to hide the runaway slaves were "station-keepers."

Messages were sent in code between station-keepers. Can you decipher the true meaning of this one?

Mr. C. B. C.

Dear Sir,
    By tomorrow evening's mail you will receive two volumes of the "Irrepressible Conflict" bound in black. After perusal, please forward and oblige.

Yours truly,
G. W. W.

The web of escape routes was called the "line" or the "track." The final destinations where the slaves arrived in freedom were known as "terminals." The use of these railroad words confused many people. Some Americans thought that there really were trains travelling in underground tunnels all the way from the southern states to Canada!

Several Canadian towns and cities became terminals on the Underground Railroad. One of the most important was Amherstburg in the southwest part of present-day Ontario. Since it was located at the narrowest point of the Detroit River, it was even possible to swim across the river to freedom. Other important terminals were Port Burwell and Port Stanley on Lake Erie. On Lake Ontario, Toronto, Hamilton, and Kingston were terminals. In Niagara, both St. Catharines and Niagara-on-the-Lake were ends of the line. Sometimes conductors in Chicago put Black refugees on steamers heading for the ports of Collingwood or Owen Sound on Georgian Bay. Passengers coming through New England were sent to Saint John, Halifax, or Montreal.

It is estimated that by 1850, 15 000 to 20 000 runaway slaves had fled to Canada by way of the Underground Railroad. In 1865, all American slaves were freed. About half the Black refugees in Canada eventually returned to the United States. The other Black settlers remained in their adopted country.

Like other immigrants of this period, many former slaves who came by the Underground Railroad became farmers. They

American slaves escape to Canada by way of the Underground Railroad.

often faced racism and were shut out of local society. However, they formed their own strong communities and established farms, schools, and churches.

The most successful self-supporting Black community in Canada was Buxton, near Chatham, Ontario. It was founded in 1849 by the Reverend William King. Freed and fugitive slaves settled on 1720 ha of land. Under King's direction, the settlement prospered. It had a post office, combined sawmill and gristmill, brick yard, and several small industries. Within 10 years, Buxton had reached a population of 1200. Descendants of the first settlers still live in the area.

Profile
Harriet Tubman

Harriet Tubman was born a slave. She escaped to Canada on the Underground Railroad and settled in St. Catharines, Ontario in 1851. Tubman chose St. Catharines as her headquarters because a large number of Blacks had made their homes there. Also, it was a short distance across the Niagara River to the United States.

Harriet Tubman made many secret journeys to the slave-holding areas in the United States to escort fugitive slaves to Canada. As a "conductor," she helped hundreds of slaves, including her sister and brothers. She never lost a "passenger" and none of the people she helped was ever recaptured. Slave owners offered a $40 000 reward for her capture. This would be equivalent to $1 million today. Although Tubman could not read or write, she was clever enough to outwit her pursuers. The people she helped called her "Moses," after the biblical figure who also led slaves to freedom.

During the American Civil War, Harriet Tubman was a nurse and later a spy and scout for the Union army. After slavery was abolished in the United States, she returned there and used her skills and influence to bring attention to the rights of women. She also established a shelter for elderly Blacks and those living with poverty.

ACTIVITIES

DIRECTLY STATED IDEAS AND INFORMATION

1. What was the Underground Railroad?

2. Who was Harriet Tubman?

INDIRECTLY STATED IDEAS AND INFORMATION

3. Pretend you are a runaway slave coming from Portsmouth, Virginia. Using the map provided, describe the route you would take.

4. Explain why slave owners offered such a high reward for the capture of Harriet Tubman.

MAKING CONNECTIONS

5. Explain how each feature that is set apart from the text is related to the topic of the Underground Railroad. Describe why you think the information the features contain is not included in the body of the text.

WRITING EXTENSION

Using information from this selection, write a one-paragraph description of the Underground Railroad that could be used as a brief encyclopedia entry. Make sure your paragraph contains both an introductory and a concluding sentence. Remember that encyclopedia entries contain factual information only, not opinions.

READING STRATEGY

Scan the pages of this textbook feature. Look at the title, the headings, the notes in the margin, and the visuals. Then *predict* what you think "Changing the World" will be about. After you have read through the selection, look back at your prediction. How accurate was it?

VOCABULARY PREVIEW

◆ boycott
◆ deprived
◆ bonded
◆ Bonded Labor Liberation Front
◆ spokesperson
◆ import

Changing the World

❖ by Sharon Sterling and Steve Powrie

When we work to find solutions to problems, we sometimes find that the issues are more complicated than they might seem at first. One issue like this is child labour.

Some people think that we should **boycott** goods produced by children. Boycotting is when people agree not to buy something to show that they disagree with something the company is doing. Because boycotting affects the profits a company makes, it can be a powerful way to get companies to change the way they do things.

Is boycotting the best solution to the problem of child labour? In this section, you can investigate the issue and find out why it's not so simple.

Pakistan is a low-income country in Asia. What does this photo show you about life for some people in Pakistan? What do you need to remember when you see only one photograph of a country?

Iqbal Masih's Story

For centuries, children around the world have worked in conditions that have ruined their health, shortened their lives, and deprived them of the chance to get an education and to lead a normal life as adults. People have always known about this. Some people have even tried to do something to improve the situation for children. In our times, though, one 10-year-old boy made the world really pay attention to this problem. His name was Iqbal Masih.

Iqbal Masih was born to a low-income family in Pakistan. When he was four years old his father needed money. In exchange for a loan of approximately $12, Iqbal went to work for the local carpet manufacturer. The idea was that Iqbal would work to pay off the loan. This is called **bonded** labour—the worker is not free to leave the job.

In the factory, Iqbal joined other children working in harsh conditions. He was chained to a loom where he made carpets. The air he breathed was filled with dust from the carpet wool. Often, his fingers were cut by the sharp tool used to trim the wool. When this happened, the cut finger was dipped in hot oil to stop the bleeding.

Iqbal worked six days a week, 13 hours a day. He was given just enough food to keep him alive. If he made a mistake, he was beaten. Over time, the factory owner kept adding interest, fines,

The life Iqbal led as a bonded labourer is not unusual. The International Labour Organization estimates that there are 15 million bonded child labourers in India alone.

Some of the goods made by children that are imported into Canada are running shoes, sports equipment (soccer balls, baseballs), carpets, and clothing.

This photograph shows a child working in a carpet factory similar to the one Iqbal worked in. Pakistan has a tropical climate, so it's very hot in a factory like this. Usually there are no windows to open for fresh air—this is to keep bugs from getting in and damaging the carpets. Can you imagine what it would be like to work in a factory like this?

UNICEF reports that about 50 000 children in Pakistan lost their jobs because of threats of boycotts, while about 1.5 million families in India no longer receive income from their children.

In 1994, Iqbal received a "Youth in Action" award for his work in human rights. In his speech when he received the award he said, "I appeal to you that you stop people from using children as bonded labourers because the children need to use a pen rather than the instruments of child labour." What do you think he meant?

and other charges to Iqbal's father's loan. The debt became so high that no matter how long Iqbal worked, he could never pay it off.

For six years, Iqbal survived life at the factory. Then, when he was 10, he came in contact with a group called the Bonded Labor Liberation Front (BLLF). The group helped him get away from his owner. Because of his difficult life, Iqbal was small for his age, and he had trouble breathing and pain in his fingers. None of these things stopped him from working with the BLLF, though, and he helped at least 3000 children forced into labour in Pakistan to gain their freedom.

Eventually Iqbal travelled around the world, speaking to groups about the life of child labourers. One of the most important things he talked about was the need for all children to get an education. Iqbal became a well-known spokesperson for children's rights and won awards for his work.

Tragically, when he was 12, Iqbal was shot and killed while riding a bicycle near his home. Some people believed he was murdered by factory owners who were against his work, although there was no evidence to prove this. Iqbal's death touched the hearts of people all over the world.

No Easy Answers

Iqbal inspired many people to take action on the issue of bonded child labourers. Politicians in the governments of the United States and Germany spoke out and began working to make it illegal to import goods made by child labourers. Many people started boycotting products made by children.

The carpet manufacturers decided they'd better pay attention. They started firing child workers. For many children, though, this didn't solve the problem. Instead, they were forced to look for other jobs. Many of these jobs, such as crushing stone and working with metal, were worse than the jobs in the factories and paid even lower wages. So while people had good intentions, the results often made matters worse.

Iqbal

Better Understanding

In time, people realized that they had to look at the reasons why children need to work in the first place. Families don't make their children work because they don't love them or don't want them—they make their children work because they need the income. People interviewing child labourers found that some children were proud to be helping their families. For many, life in the factory was better than staying home and starving.

It turned out that this was a complicated problem that needed more solutions than just stopping child labour. One solution was for organizations to provide families with a small income or loan to replace the income of a child who stops working. Another solution was to provide schools to educate children so that they could get jobs in the future. So far, these solutions have had good results in communities where they have been tried.

ACTIVITIES

DIRECTLY STATED IDEAS AND INFORMATION

1. Why has Iqbal had to work since he was four?

2. According to the text, why are boycotts not necessarily the best solution to the problem of child labour? What other solutions does it describe?

INDIRECTLY STATED IDEAS AND INFORMATION

3. Why do you think Iqbal was killed?

4. In Canada, children are often expected to help out at home. How is child labour different from this kind of work?

MAKING CONNECTIONS

5. What do the photographs add to your understanding of the issue of child labour?

WRITING EXTENSION

Write a summary of this selection in 200 words or less. Include the main ideas and events from each subsection.

READING STRATEGY

*Try the **Pairs Read** strategy for this selection.*
1. *Find a partner and decide who will be the reader and who will be the coach.*
2. *The reader reads the first paragraph aloud to the coach. The coach then uses his or her own words to summarize the main idea and supporting details of that paragraph back to the reader. The coach may ask questions of the reader to clarify anything he or she didn't understand.*
3. *Switch roles for the next paragraph. Continue the process until you have read the whole selection. If you come to any visuals, whoever is the reader at that time must explain what is being shown.*

VOCABULARY PREVIEW

- assailant
- algebraic formulas
- skeptical
- itinerary
- accommodations
- rehabilitation
- frivolous
- material wealth
- desperation
- devastate

It Starts with Me

❖ by Craig Kielburger

I usually read the comics in the *Toronto Star* each morning before I go to school. But one day in April 1995, a front-page story stopped me. There was a picture of a smiling boy, his arm upraised. His name was Iqbal Masih. He looked to be about my age at the time—12. According to the article, he had worked in a carpet factory in Pakistan for most of his life. Then he escaped and travelled in his country and the West, speaking out against child labour. The previous Sunday, he had been shot dead by an unknown assailant.

Suddenly, everything seemed terribly still. *Why was this kid murdered?* I wondered. *Why did he have to work in a factory?*

The most my parents asked of me was to take out the garbage, mow the lawn, and get good grades. My cereal went soggy as I read on. I never got to the comics that morning.

All through the school day, I couldn't stop thinking about Iqbal. Here I was memorizing algebraic formulas while somewhere kids were tying wool into tiny knots from dawn to dusk. How would I have handled it if I were in their place? The article had said that Iqbal's parents, who were extremely poor, had sent him to work in the factory when he was just four. Some suspected that factory owners, angry with Iqbal for exposing their abuses, might be behind his killing.

I went to the library and looked for information on child-labour practices. Most of the articles were about the often terrible conditions in Europe and North America in the early part of the century. What about nowadays?

Then I heard about a group called Youth Action Network. I called and spoke to Alam Rahman, a recent college graduate. His father had immigrated to Canada from Bangladesh. "If things had been a little different," he said, "I could have been a child labourer."

So could I, I thought. If I'd been born in an earlier time or if my family had been poor—it could have been me denied the chance to get an education.

"I think there should be a children's organization fighting child labour," I said. "Kids speaking for kids."

"That's a great idea, Craig. Why don't you start one?"

Easy to say. But how could I convince my classmates? Would they think I was weird?

The next day in homeroom, I passed around copies of the article and told the class what I'd learned. On their faces was the same shock I had felt when I first read the article. "I thought maybe some of us could get together and see if there was anything we could do. Who's interested?" A dozen hands shot up.

We met at my house that evening. As we talked about child labour, I felt this intense connection—both to my classmates and to the kids on whose behalf we had come together. One of the clippings told of a rally of over 250 children in Delhi, India. "Free the children," they had chanted. We would take up their cry. Our group had a name.

FTC put together youth fair displays and spoke at schools and churches. We did a lot of research and sent petitions to foreign governments, including one with 3000 names to India urging the release of political prisoner Kailash Satyarthi, a leading crusader against child labour.

By the time school started again the next fall, FTC had something of a reputation. Some kids resented our opposition to brand-name sneakers and jeans made by child labourers. "Do you want us to make our own clothes? Isn't that child labour?" one boy cracked. Some kids were skeptical about the articles I showed them about child labour. "How do you know all this is true?" a 10th-grade girl asked. "Have you seen these kids for yourself?"

"No, but I hope to someday," I replied weakly.

Then one day, Alam told me he was planning to spend a year in Asia. "I'll take you along. This could be your chance to meet some of the workers." My parents trusted and respected Alam. But they didn't even allow me to ride the subway to downtown Toronto by myself. They wanted detailed explanations of Alam's itinerary, whom I would meet, what safety precautions we would take. I began to get e-mails from contacts around the world, offering accommodations, wondering when I would be coming. My parents were being won over.

That fall, I was invited to speak at a convention of the Ontario Federation of Labour. I was a nervous wreck, an eighth grader speaking to over 2000 adults. But I started with the story of Iqbal and soon found my voice. By the end of the evening, $150 000 had been pledged to help build a rehabilitation centre and school for freed child labourers. When the OFL spokesperson raised my arm in the air to thunderous applause, I couldn't help but remember that original photo of Iqbal, his arm raised in the same gesture. I just stood there with a giant grin on my face, knowing that somewhere Iqbal was smiling, too.

I left home on December 10 and joined Alam in Dhaka, Bangladesh. I wanted to meet as many working kids as I could. In Bangkok, Thailand, we saw really young kids being exploited in the sex trade. I talked to 10-year-old boys who had quit school to work 15-hour days to help support their families and realized how frivolous my hours spent playing ball would seem to them. "It's easy to tell these countries that these kids should not have to work under such horrible conditions," a Western relief agency official told me. "But remember, a big part of the problem is us. We buy this stuff. Instead of merely being a market for these products, the West needs to help find solutions to the underlying poverty in the Third World."

He was right. I came from a society that prided itself on its material wealth. I thought of all the video games piled on my desk, the clothes in my closet. Was I part of the problem, too?

In Pakistan, I talked to a boy making bricks. He had been sold into labour by his grandfather to pay a debt. "Would you like to go to school?" I asked him.

"What is school?" he asked me.

All around me, I saw the poverty that drove people to such desperation. I figured the choice was pretty clear in many cases: work or starve.

I had read so much about child labourers, and yet face-to-face I was amazed at how many were lively, spirited kids. They weren't waiting for anyone to save them. They were making the best of conditions that would devastate most adults.

We found a girl with a ribbon in her hair in a run-down building in Madras, India. With no protection for her hands, she was taking apart used syringes so the plastic could be recycled. "Sometimes I cut myself," she said, "but I always wash with water."

What's the point of all this, God? I wondered. *I keep meeting suffering kids, and I can't do anything for them.*

Then in Varanasi, India, we were contacted by Kailash Satyarthi, the man whose release FTC had petitioned for months earlier. He had been let go, and recently he had led a raid on a carpet factory, setting free 22 children. He invited us to help see them safely home.

We crammed into two Jeeps. The boy next to me was about eight, and his name was Munnilal. "I was given no money by my master," he told me. "I was hit again and again." The Jeep jostled as we drove down into a creek. Then it got stuck in the mud. Everyone jumped out and pushed it. When we reached shore, I stood there, exhausted and soaking wet. Munnilal took a blanket from around his shoulders and held it out to me. "Here, you'll catch cold," he said.

"No, you keep it," I said, staring at this child who had been through more hardship in eight years of life than I would ever go through. In that instant, I understood. Munnilal had almost nothing, but what he had, he offered me. For most of the kids

I met, all I could do was share their stories and raise money, but I would do it as sincerely as Munnilal had offered me that blanket.

We got back into the Jeeps and drove the children to their villages. When Munnilal's mother saw him, she hugged him, weeping. "You are so thin," she said.

"When I hurt most," he said to her, "I saw you in my dreams."

"I saw you in my dreams, too," she answered.

I thought of my mom waiting for my calls, the way she was marking off each day of my trip on the calendar. Suddenly, I felt terribly homesick.

But there was one more stop to make, the one I had thought about most. In Muridke, Pakistan, we walked down the route of Iqbal's funeral procession. "The day Iqbal died, a thousand other Iqbals were born," a girl had said at his funeral. I was grateful to be one of them.

ACTIVITIES

DIRECTLY STATED IDEAS AND INFORMATION

1. What story distracted Kielburger from reading the comics? What caused him to keep reading?

2. Give three examples from the text that illustrate the situations of child labourers.

INDIRECTLY STATED IDEAS AND INFORMATION

3. How are Canadians part of the problem of child labour?

4. Explain in your own words what Munnilal's offer of the blanket shows about him.

MAKING CONNECTIONS

5. What can we do in Canada to improve the lives of children in other countries? How can we "think globally and act locally"?

WRITING EXTENSION

Choose an issue you are concerned about, and create a bulleted list of positive things you could do to help change the situation.

READING STRATEGY

Images often give the viewer a strong emotional reaction. What emotion do you feel when you look at the image in this poster?

VOCABULARY PREVIEW

◆ helplessness
◆ gnawing
◆ frustrating
◆ ongoing
◆ doubting

A Call to Volunteer

How some in Toronto plan their next meal

ACTIVITIES

DIRECTLY STATED IDEAS AND INFORMATION

1. List the components of this poster. What takes up the majority of the space?

2. According to the poster, what are three different ways that people feel the effects of helplessness?

INDIRECTLY STATED IDEAS AND INFORMATION

3. What message is suggested by the hands?

4. What did you notice first? How does the poster use contrast to get your attention?

MAKING CONNECTIONS

5. How does the approach taken in this poster compare with that of other posters that encourage people to get involved?

WRITING EXTENSION

Using your own words and details from the poster, write a paragraph explaining how people can help to fight hunger in their community.

> Never doubt that a small group of thoughtful committed citizens can change the world; indeed, it is the only thing that ever has.
>
> — *Margaret Mead (1901–1978)*
> *Anthropologist*

Four Who Make a Difference
Meet young volunteers who have changed lives for the better

❖ by Jennifer Burke Crump

Isabelle Rivard: FreeRide Snowboarding Project

With their multicoloured hair shaved close to their heads or shaped into towering mohawks, the group of 28 street kids and patients from Ottawa's Children's Hospital of Eastern Ontario mental-health ward attracted a lot of attention at the prestigious Camp Fortune skiing facility in the Gatineau Hills.

In the middle of the group stood Isabelle Rivard, their teacher and mentor. She looked just like one of the kids, and in fact, she was. Barely 17, her lips, tongue, and an eyebrow pierced, this former drug user was the sole reason a group of troubled young people were discovering snowboarding that day in January 1997.

As her eyes scanned the group, her confident, calm voice alternately encouraged and cautioned. "Take your time, don't try too much yet," she warned the more eager members. "You are going to have to do this yourself; I can't do it for you," she bluntly told others who seemed more timid.

The FreeRide Snowboarding Project takes groups of street kids to Camp Fortune every Monday for six weeks. For kids who have lived with depression, self-mutilation, suicidal behaviours, and other mental-health problems, snowboarding has proved to be a healthy way to cope with emotional trauma. "It gives them something to look forward to

and work towards," says Sarah Brandon, a co-ordinator for Youth Net/Réseau Ado, a mental-health and early-intervention program that's affiliated with Ottawa's Children's Hospital and that works with communities in both Ontario and Quebec.

No one understands this better than Isabelle. As a teen, she progressed from marijuana to hard drugs. She'd party all night and return to her home in Touraine, Quebec, to sleep the day away. She was constantly at war with her parents, who struggled to help her as the drugs drew her into a deadly spiral of depression. When it became unbearable, she would mutilate herself, scarring her arms in a vain attempt to ease her emotional pain.

After nothing else seemed to work, Isabelle's parents took her to the Children's Hospital, which had facilities for clinically depressed youths. Isabelle arrived defiant, apathetic, and adrift. While the hospital provided a safe haven, it seemed more like

a prison to her. An avid snowboarder, she craved the physical excitement and mental escape the sport gave her, though from her hospital window she couldn't even see the ski hills, much less reach them.

Then fate stepped in. In conversation one day, Youth Net's Brandon discovered Isabelle's passion for snowboarding and engineered a day on the slopes for the two of them. Isabelle's transformation amazed Brandon.

Believing others could feel the way she did on the slopes, Isabelle created the FreeRide Snowboarding Project and approached Youth Net for support. The Youth Net team, which includes a mix of youths, facilitators, and clinicians, made her a deal: Isabelle could organize the program as long as she shunned drugs and didn't try to hurt herself.

To raise funds, she asked Ottawa shop owners to donate raffle prizes, for which she sold tickets. She found snowboarding volunteers from a local high school and from Camp Fortune to help her teach the street kids and patients. Next she approached Peter Sudermann, Camp Fortune's owner, who agreed to give the kids passes and boards at ridiculously low rates.

Founded in 1997, the FreeRide Snowboarding Project received a Pan-Commonwealth Youth Service Award in November 2000. And Isabelle? "Snowboarding put me back on my feet," she says. Today she is a happy, self-confident young woman balancing full- and part-time jobs while living in Whistler, B.C., a stone's throw from the ski hills—where she snowboards daily.

Lance Relland: Aboriginal Bone Marrow Registries

At 16, Lance Relland was a promising dancer with the Royal Winnipeg Ballet School. But in July 1996, shortly before he turned 17, the auburn-haired, brown-eyed Edmontonian was informed he had a rare, deadly form of acute lymphoblastic leukemia—and four to seven months to live.

Lance had no intention of giving in to illness any more than he had given in to other challenges he'd faced in his young life—whether it was coming to terms with his Métis heritage or mastering classical ballet.

Still, doctors were vague about Lance's type of leukemia and its treatment. "I need to find out everything I can about this disease. I need to know what can be done," Lance told his mother.

While searching for information on the Internet, he found references to a monoclonal antibody against leukemia cells that had been discovered by researchers at the University of Minnesota. This antibody treatment seemed to be working for people with his type of leukemia. It was available only in the United States, however, and the provincial government would not pay for it.

Undaunted, Lance's family and friends started a foundation in September 1996 and raised more than $100 000 to cover the costs of his treatment at the Fairview-University Medical Center in Minneapolis. Lance received the monoclonal antibody there and in October had a bone-marrow transplant from his brother. Four and a half years later, Lance remains cancer-free.

During his stay in hospital and while recovering as an outpatient, Lance spent hours talking to other cancer patients. Many, he found out, lacked basic knowledge about their illness and had no idea how to locate needed information. He also met kids whose parents and doctors had been unable to find matching bone-marrow donors. *I want something good to come from the bad things that have happened to me*, he decided as he flew home to Alberta.

On his return, Lance persuaded the foundation set up in his name to keep going, and to make patient education its focus. The result: The Lance Relland Medical Foundation now provides to cancer and other patients in Edmonton access to Internet documents as well as a $200 000 medical library provided by an anonymous donor. It also helps fund patients seeking medical treatment not covered by the Alberta government.

But for Lance, this still wasn't enough. During his research, he had discovered that the aboriginal population had only 1 percent representation on Canadian and U.S. bone-marrow lists. Ideal donors are found first within a patient's family, then his or her ethnic group. So in 1998 Lance set up the Aboriginal Bone Marrow Registries, which accept donors from any ethnic group in North America but focus on recruiting Indian, Métis, and Inuit people.

Lance has since travelled to reserves and high schools across Alberta to convince people to join the registries and to push for a healthy lifestyle. "One illegal drug injection or exposure to HIV or Hepatitis C will prevent you from donating," he tells his audience, "and someday, someone in your family might need you." Lance's aboriginal registries now list over 800 donors.

In 1999 Lance began his studies in medicine at the University of California, Riverside, and he continues to support the foundation and registries he started.

ACTIVITIES

DIRECTLY STATED IDEAS AND INFORMATION

1. Explain in your own words how the FreeRide Snowboarding Project began.

2. How did the Lance Relland Medical Foundation begin?

INDIRECTLY STATED IDEAS AND INFORMATION

3. Both projects began as a way to meet one person's needs, but have expanded to help the greater community. Explain how this happened in each case.

MAKING CONNECTIONS

4. Why is someone with Isabelle's background an excellent mentor for young people trying to beat a drug addiction?

VOCABULARY
PREVIEW

◆ integrate   ◆ hectic

◆ interact   ◆ mischievous

◆ tolerance

Amy Brandon: Lunch Buddies

Haliburton, Ontario, teenager Amy Brandon had known Russell Snoddon since they were both in kindergarten, where Amy's mother, a special-education assistant, would come in to help the young boy with Down's syndrome. By the time Amy and Russell reached high school, the boy was a frequent visitor to the Brandon household. "Let's play cops and robbers," Russell would plead, and Amy, playing the bad guy, would let Russell arrest her, over and over.

In 1998 Amy heard about a new program at Haliburton Highlands Secondary School called Lunch Buddies—a program that paired high-school students with special-education students in an attempt to integrate them into high-school life. Before the program, the special-ed students would often hang around in a separate room and watch movies at lunchtime. Many students tended to avoid them. *They just don't know how to interact with them*, Amy realized.

Inspired by her experience with Russell, Amy volunteered with Lunch Buddies, and after one year she took it over. She went from class to class explaining the program and urging her fellow students to join. She held meetings to give other volunteers a chance to ask questions and raise concerns. "What am I supposed to do when she won't stop hugging me?" asked one volunteer, clearly concerned about the invasion of her personal space but worried about hurting her buddy's feelings. Amy remembered Russell's affection. "Just tell her calmly and gently that you don't like it," Amy replied. "She'll understand."

With Amy's guidance, Lunch Buddies grew from 10 volunteers to over 40. Suddenly, there was a new attitude of acceptance and tolerance in the school. The special-ed kids became more confident and mixed freely with the other students.

An acquaintance of Amy's thought J. Douglas Hodgson Elementary, right next to the high school, could use a similar program. So when the teachers at Hodgson gave Amy the go-ahead, she approached her Lunch Buddies volunteers. "Does anyone want to help?" Ten students offered their assistance.

Lunch hour soon became a completely different experience for the special-education kids at Hodgson. There were high-school students in the playground helping to organize games, while Amy scheduled pizza parties and days when volunteers helped the children bake cookies and make crafts. During one hectic cookie-baking session, Andrew, a cute, mischievous boy with Down's syndrome, solemnly looked up at Amy and gave a tug on her clothing. Amy bent down to his level and he kissed her cheek, whispering softly, "Thank you."

The impact of the Lunch Buddies program on the community as a whole was nothing short of amazing, says Cheryl Anderson, executive director of the Haliburton County Association for Community Living. The special-education kids are having a great time interacting with people who aren't adults. The high-school students know they are making a difference. And a new generation of young volunteers is being created.

VOCABULARY PREVIEW

- chord
- liberated
- emaciated
- typhus
- rapt
- grudge
- habitual
- adjacent
- ridiculed
- initiated
- innovative

Joe Hooper: Wheels in Motion

When Joe Hooper of Victoria was 13, he would probably have been labelled an at-risk youth. His 16-year-old sister had run away from home when he was ten, his family was facing financial difficulty, and his parents' marriage was breaking up. The red-haired, freckle-faced youth had moved from school to school as his parents tried to deal with their problems. At each new school, Joe tried to fit in or get the attention of his peers—most often by doing what he calls "really stupid things": lighting stink bombs and experimenting with alcohol and drugs.

Then, in Grade 12, a teacher took Joe and his classmates to listen to a group of Holocaust survivors. That day in April 1994, something one of them said struck a chord in Joe.

Dr. Peter Gary, a Hungarian emigré, had lost most of his family during World War II. "In 1941 my mother and I were taken to the forest and the Nazis machine-gunned us. My mother saved me by throwing herself on me. I was 17." Gary spent the next three and a half years in concentration camps before he was finally liberated, emaciated and dying of typhus. "Do you think I'm angry?" he asked his rapt audience. "I'm not. You must go through life with your hand held out in friendship, not anger."

Here was a man who had been through hell but wasn't angry and held no grudge, thought Joe in wonder. Then he reflected on his own anger—at his past, his family— and his selfish behaviour, his attempts to get attention. *Everything is not about me*, he realized.

Inspired, he thought of ways he could reach out to others, just as this man had. He began making phone calls. He landed first at a day camp for intellectually challenged children. Then he volunteered at an English- as-a-second-language centre, where he helped newly arrived immigrants settle in. Then later, during his second year at the University of Victoria, he took a part-time job with the Saanich recreation services department and its youth activity centre.

When other staff members would lose patience and want to kick one of the kids out of the centre, Joe would think, *What can I do to keep him here*? Kenny, an unemployed 18-year-old alcoholic and habitual thief, was someone the centre had banned when its staff could no longer cope with his drunken behaviour. Joe learned that Kenny was interested in weight lifting and got him a pass to a local gym, where the two would meet and talk. Persuaded by Joe to enter a rehab program for his

drinking, Kenny was ultimately accepted back at the centre and went on to find a full-time job.

Having mentored Kenny and others, Joe would often hang out at the skateboard park adjacent to the youth-activity centre and a local convenience store, talking to teenagers who gathered there. He began to notice one young man who hung around but was never part of any group. Max, Joe discovered, was a loner with no self-confidence who was frequently ridiculed.

One day Max met Joe cycling around on his mountain bike. Joe offered to let him try it. "I never learned to ride a bike," the boy replied with some embarrassment. Joe was stunned—the kid was 17!

Over the next few months, Joe and his friend Greg taught the boy to ride, then found him a secondhand mountain bike. At the Hartland Mountain Biking Park outside Victoria, they put the new biker to the test, and Max proved to be a natural. "Today Max is a sponsored mountain-bike racer in national competitions," Joe says with pride.

Backed by the Saanich police, who donated the bikes, and employees of a local cycle shop who volunteered to repair them and provide training, Joe went on to raise funds to transport kids from the youth activity centre to the mountains.

The program he initiated last year, called Wheels in Motion, became an outstanding success, with many young people learning better social skills and developing self-confidence. And although Joe now lives in Ottawa, his program is still running.

Young volunteers like Isabelle, Lance, Amy, and Joe are growing in number. Statistics Canada reports that between 1987 and 1997, youth volunteer rates nearly doubled at a time when the rates for most other age groups remained relatively stable. "Despite what some mainstream media would have you believe, there is a strong social conscience among youths," says Steve Carroll, a program manager at Volunteer Canada.

Many still volunteer through existing, traditional organizations like the United Way, the Canadian Cancer Society, and the Heart and Stroke Foundation. But a growing number of teens are striking out on their own, creating solutions for their communities' problems in ways that are both innovative and highly successful.

Leslie Evans, executive director of the Youth Volunteer Corps of Canada, says the best ideas often come from the kids themselves, whether it's a fashion show for seniors in St. John's, Newfoundland, or a blanket drive for the homeless in Nanaimo, B.C. Across Canada young people are organizing soup kitchens or toy drives, tutoring children, raking lawns for seniors, cleaning up parks. And our communities are the better for it.

ACTIVITIES

DIRECTLY STATED IDEAS AND INFORMATION

1. Explain how one girl's interest and experience inspired others in the Lunch Buddies program.

2. Explain how Joe found purpose for himself by helping others with the Wheels in Motion program.

INDIRECTLY STATED IDEAS AND INFORMATION

3. What types of activities are suitable for the Lunch Buddies program?

4. Why did hearing the story of the Holocaust survivor change Joe's outlook on his own life?

MAKING CONNECTIONS

5. Both Lunch Buddies and Wheels in Motion depend on education for the program to succeed. Explain what they teach.

WRITING EXTENSION

Write a newspaper article about one of the four teens profiled in this selection. Choose a specific event related to his or her story as the focus of your article. Put important information near the beginning of the article. Remember that a reporter does not give his or her personal opinions on a story. However, you may include quotations that express an opinion.

READING STRATEGY
Look over the two elements of this selection besides the main text. What purpose does each serve?

Bright Idea

❖ by Guenther Zuern

VOCABULARY PREVIEW

◆ distressed
◆ electricity
◆ light-emitting diodes
◆ prestigious
◆ visionaries

Made in Canada

Canadians are inventive people. Here are some of Canada's most famous inventions and inventors.

Basketball
invented by James Naismith in 1891.

Canada Dry Ginger Ale
John A. McLaughlin in 1907.

Electric light bulb
Henry Woodward in 1874; he sold the patent to Thomas Edison.

Electric streetcar
John Joseph Wright in 1883.

Insulin
(as a treatment for diabetes): invented by Doctors Banting, Best, Collip, and McCleod in 1922.

Heart pacemaker
Dr. John A. Hopps in 1950.

Plastic garbage bag
Harry Wasylyk in 1950.

Standard time
Sir Sanford Fleming in 1878.

Snowblower
Arthur Sicard in 1925.

Snowmobile
Joseph-Armand Bombardier in 1922.

Telephone
Alexander Graham Bell in 1876.

Walkie-talkie
Donald L. Hings in 1942.

Wireless radio
Reginald A. Fessenden in 1900.

Zipper
Gideon Sundback in 1913.

Dave Irvine-Halliday is an electrical engineer and professor at the University of Calgary. In 1997, he travelled in a remote part of Nepal. He was distressed to see that children there had little opportunity to learn to read and write. During the day, many children had to work in the rice fields. At night, studying was difficult because few homes had electric lights.

When he returned to Canada, Irvine-Halliday was still upset by the thought of children learning in the dark. He wondered if there was some way to bring light to those children and millions of others in the world who live with no electricity.

Irvine-Halliday began to search for an inexpensive, reliable light source. He experimented with light-emitting diodes or LEDs. These are used in alarm clocks and remote controls. Eventually, he developed a lamp that provides enough light for a child to read by, but uses very little electricity. Using the low-energy diode lamps and solar panels as a power source, Irvine-Halliday devised a safe, cheap, and dependable lighting system. The system can light an entire village with less energy than it takes to power a 100-watt light bulb.

Irvine-Halliday established the Light Up the World Foundation to bring the system to remote villages around the world. He had to use his family's entire life savings to support the Foundation. So far, he has installed lighting systems in 1000 homes in Africa, South Asia, and Central America.

In October 2002, Irvine-Halliday was recognized for his efforts. He received the prestigious (US) $100 000 Rolex Award for Enterprise. This award is given to visionaries who improve the world. Irvine-Halliday will use the award to install more lighting systems. His goal is to bring light to a million people by 2005.

ACTIVITIES

DIRECTLY STATED IDEAS AND INFORMATION

1. After his travels in Nepal, what particularly bothered Dave Irvine-Halliday?

2. What funding has he used to support the Light Up the World Foundation?

INDIRECTLY STATED IDEAS AND INFORMATION

3. How do you know that these lights are very economical?

4. Why do you think these lights are not available in Canada?

MAKING CONNECTIONS

5. What do you think are the five most helpful inventions on the Made in Canada list? Defend your choices.

WRITING EXTENSION

Write a four-sentence summary of the article. Remember to identify the main ideas and to use your own words as much as possible.

I just wish people would realize
that anything is possible if you try;
dreams are made if people try.

— *Terry Fox (1958–1981)*
Athlete

READING STRATEGY

*Before you read this selection, **scan** it to find out how the expression "the real McCoy" came into use. Pass your eyes briefly over the text, searching for the key words "real McCoy." You can use this method to find information to answer some of the activities as well.*

VOCABULARY PREVIEW

- ◆ seize
- ◆ lubrication
- ◆ self-regulating
- ◆ ingenious
- ◆ spent
- ◆ patented
- ◆ "the real McCoy"
- ◆ established
- ◆ durable
- ◆ progressive

The Real McCoy

❖ by Bev Spencer

In the 1800s train travel had a big drawback. Steam engine parts would overheat and seize up, if used non-stop. The parts needed lubrication—oil to help the moving parts run smoothly—so trains had to make frequent stops to let the fireman drip oil onto every moving part, up and down the train and in the engine. Impatient passengers had to wait . . . and wait . . . and wait.

Enter Elijah McCoy. McCoy's parents had been slaves* in the United States. They escaped to Canada in 1837 so their children could be educated—slaves were not allowed to read or write—and McCoy was born in Ontario, in freedom. Later his parents sent him to Scotland to become a trained engineer. But after his return to the U.S., the best job he could find in Ypsilanti, Michigan, as a Black man, was as a train fireman/oilman. He spent his days shovelling coal into the fire

chamber of the steam engine, and running up and down the train, hand-lubricating moveable parts. McCoy saw the need for automatic lubricators, and worked in his shop at home for two years to create a self-regulating lubricating oil cup. It used steam pressure in cylinders to operate a valve and release the oil—a big improvement over any other lubricators at the time.

McCoy's system was ingenious. The cup that held the oil was built in as part of the steam cylinder. Oil could flow through a hollow rod attached to the base of the cup when the engine's steam pressure opened up the valve at the top of the rod. All this happened automatically as the steam engine's pistons moved up through the cylinder. So the engine regularly released oil from the cup to lubricate itself under normal running conditions. A year later McCoy

---

*   Please refer to the footnote on page 189.

changed his design so the oil would be released when the steam was spent. McCoy patented his oil cup in 1872. In later years he patented over 50 lubricating systems.

At first, white engineers were not interested in McCoy's invention. But, installed on trains under McCoy's supervision, the lubricator worked perfectly, and revolutionized railroad travel. The time needed for train travel was cut dramatically because no stops for lubrication were needed. Word spread. Soon other trains installed the lubricator, and within 10 years it was used in mines and factories as well as on locomotives.

There were imitations of McCoy's device, but they didn't work nearly as well as his version, so people were soon asking for "the real McCoy." The new expression entered common speech, to mean "the best."

To find the time to work on his own inventions, Elijah McCoy moved with his wife to Detroit, Michigan, in 1882, and established his own company. His 87 other inventions include a folding ironing board, designs for tires and tire treads, a more durable rubber shoe heel, a lawn sprinkler, and improved versions of his oil cup. Today, variations of McCoy's oil cup are still used in factories, mines, navy ships, construction machinery, and space vehicles.

McCoy was a great engineering inventor. His advice to children was simple: "Stay in school. Be progressive. Work hard."

ACTIVITIES

DIRECTLY STATED IDEAS AND INFORMATION

1. When did Elijah McCoy's parents escape to Canada? Why?

2. How did McCoy's lubricating system improve railroad travel?

INDIRECTLY STATED IDEAS AND INFORMATION

3. Why were white engineers not interested in McCoy's invention at first?

4. What do you think McCoy meant by "Be progressive"?

MAKING CONNECTIONS

5. What qualities do you think you would need to be an inventor? What do you think pushes people to invent?

WRITING EXTENSION

What information do you think would be needed on a patent application form? Create a form that could be used to register patents.

READING STRATEGY

Before reading this selection, complete this sentence: I do (or do not) think hockey is a dangerous sport because . . .

VOCABULARY PREVIEW

◆ protective

◆ experiment

◆ suffered

◆ opposed

◆ interfere

◆ gruesome

◆ extent

Safer Hockey

❖ by Bev Spencer

"He shoots! He scores! *Ouch!* The goalie took it in the face! He's down. Medics are on the ice . . ."

This scene was all too common in ice hockey matches until the widespread use of protective goalie face masks. A few goaltenders experimented with masks decades before the face mask would be accepted, including Montreal Maroons player Clint Benedict around 1930. But masks never caught on until Jacques Plante wore one. The modern hockey face mask has become standard protection for players of all ages . . . from kids' to professional teams, because of two Canadians. Today, fans collect pictures of the colourful, varied masks their favourite goalies wear.

By 1959, Jacques Plante, an NHL All-Star goalie, had been injured in the face many times. Fast-travelling pucks had broken his jaw, both cheekbones and his nose. He had already had 200 stitches in his face. He had even suffered a hairline fracture of the skull. Plante decided that was enough. He made his own rigid goalie mask, with some help from Fiberglas Canada.

Plante was afraid fans might think less of him for wearing a mask. And his coach opposed the mask, so at first he only wore it during practices. But after a puck gave him a big gash in his upper lip during a game, he refused to return to the ice without the mask. He proved it didn't interfere with his playing by winning the game. After that, Plante decided to wear it for every game. When his team, the Montreal Canadiens, won the Stanley Cup for the third time in a row, Plante was in the net and the mask was on.

Plante led the way by *wearing* his mask. Toronto-born Dr. Tom Pashby worked to *make* both the mask and helmets standard hockey equipment. A keen hockey fan, Pashby never missed a game at Toronto's Maple Leaf Gardens. His friend George Parsons was playing for the Leafs in 1939 when he took a hockey stick in the face and was blinded in one eye. The cause? Highsticking. Parsons lost both the eye and his hockey career that night.

Pashby had nearly finished medical school when he witnessed this gruesome accident, and he was shaken. He became an ophthalmologist, or eye doctor. Soon he was stitching up players after the games at the Gardens. His own son suffered a head injury during a house league hockey game, but recovered. After another player in the majors was blinded in 1973, the Canadian Ophthalmological Society knew who could help. Pashby prepared a report on the extent of eye injuries in hockey. It helped change hockey rules.

In 1975 the Canadian Amateur Hockey Association (CAHA) modified the highsticking rules, making the game safer. Pashby pushed the Canadian Standards Association (CSA) for rules on protective eyewear. By 1979 all minor hockey players had to wear a CSA-approved face-protector-and-helmet combination. It was the first safety standard like it anywhere. Eye injuries in hockey were cut dramatically.

Now, no one scoffs at a hockey player in a helmet, or a goalie with a helmet and face mask. And highsticking is not allowed. Canada led the way, and Pashby continued to push for eye protection in other sports.

ACTIVITIES

DIRECTLY STATED IDEAS AND INFORMATION

1. What is an ophthalmologist?

2. Who are the two Canadians who helped to make face masks acceptable in the hockey world?

INDIRECTLY STATED IDEAS AND INFORMATION

3. Explain why fans in 1959 might think less of a goalie for wearing a mask.

4. In paragraph five, two words, "wearing" and "make," are written in italics. Explain the purpose of using this type of font here.

MAKING CONNECTIONS

5. What other inventions can you think of that have made people's lives safer? Work with a partner to create a list of the "Top Five Safety Improvements in the Last 100 Years."

WRITING EXTENSION

Write a summary of this selection in no more than 100 words.

READING STRATEGY
*Read the selection one section at a time. As you come to each subhead, **predict** what you think the next section will be about.*

Teens Make Their Own Peace

❖ by Leah Eskin

VOCABULARY PREVIEW

- ◆ plantations
- ◆ deferred
- ◆ devoted
- ◆ encounters
- ◆ universal
- ◆ underlying
- ◆ optimism
- ◆ idealism
- ◆ guarded
- ◆ befriend
- ◆ frustrated

Carlos Hernandez grew up in El Salvador. But he never had a childhood there. "At seven years old I was working in the coffee plantations from six in the morning until six in the afternoon," says Carlos, now 19. "We were living in the worst conditions that a human being can have, eating the same things day after day. I also saw dead people in the street. In my country it is not a big deal to see a person that has been tortured and thrown on the street, in the middle of the street, every day. People, even children, get used to it."

But Carlos couldn't get used to the idea that 13-year-olds like himself were being forced into the army, to fight in El Salvador's civil war. In 1984, he and his family fled to Mexico and then crept across the border into the U.S. "We didn't want to leave," says Carlos. "We were forced to leave because

of the conditions. I miss my country. I miss my people. I feel like I should be there sharing the trouble that they are going through. One day, the dream of my family is to go back."

A Dream Deferred

Until that day, Carlos has devoted himself to sharing his story with other young people. In the fall of 1986, Carlos and 62 other young victims of violence spent a month telling American high school students about their experiences. The tour was sponsored by Children of War, an organization that hopes such encounters will help rid the world of wars.

"What we do is so simple," says program director Judith Thompson.

"We get people together and they talk to each other. You begin to see that human suffering is universal. One person may have experienced war, another from a middle-class background may have experienced drugs or a suicide attempt. But there is an underlying connection between their pain. You find, buried within you, new hope, optimism, and idealism."

When the Children of War tour came to Brookline High, in Brookline, Massachusetts, it sparked that kind of idealism in Autumn Bennett. "One at a time, each of the kids started talking about their experiences in war," says Autumn, then 16. "I never thought that war was something that affected people my own age; I thought it was fought by grown men. By the end, the whole room was just crying. It was unusual to see people who are usually very guarded against each other, just opening up and crying."

A Volunteer for Peace

The experience changed her life. Autumn began to notice—and befriend—refugees who attended her own school. She started thinking about warlike conditions young people face today: drugs, gang violence, and homelessness. She helped start a local chapter of Children of War. And she spent a year between high school and college helping plan the next Children of War tour.

"I want to educate my peers," says Autumn. "I want them to know that war does affect them. If you work to change adults or change the government, you'll get frustrated. But if you work to reach other youth, you feel powerful, you don't feel alone any more."

Carlos agrees. "On the tour, I learned that it was not only me that had been through horrible things, that had pain inside. I learned about struggles in South Africa, Haiti, and Northern Ireland. Now every time I read a newspaper and see something from, say, South Africa, I feel like something over there is part of me. It is the same struggle that young people everywhere go through."

That knowledge, say both Autumn and Carlos, is the key to creating a more peaceful world. "I realized after the tour that I was a very powerful person," says Carlos. "I realized I can make change in the world."

Miracles happen when young people get together.

— *Jeanne Sauvé (1922–1993)*
Former Canadian Governer General

ACTIVITIES

DIRECTLY STATED IDEAS AND INFORMATION

1. Why did Carlos and his family leave El Salvador?

2. What approach does the Children of War tour take to creating peace?

INDIRECTLY STATED IDEAS AND INFORMATION

3. Summarize the effect the Children of War tour had on Carlos, and on Autumn.

4. How does it help the cause of peace for people to know that we have many problems in common around the world?

MAKING CONNECTIONS

5. Why do you think Autumn feels that "If you work to change adults or change the government, you'll get frustrated. But if you work to reach other youth, you feel powerful"? Do you agree with her? Explain.

WRITING EXTENSION

Find a newspaper article reporting on violence in a country outside North America. How well does the journalist manage to convey the human anguish associated with the story? Write a letter to the editor of the newspaper in which you either compliment or complain about how the article represented the human side of the story. Give specific examples to support your point of view.

Skim the selection to find out how the photo relates to the text.

Kim Phuc

❖ by David M.R.D. Spencer

- ◆ Viet Cong
- ◆ blockade
- ◆ napalm
- ◆ allies
- ◆ fortifications
- ◆ Pulitzer Prize
- ◆ instinctively
- ◆ engulfed
- ◆ elite
- ◆ special ambassador to UNESCO

Kim's life was forever changed by one horrifying moment during the Vietnam War. Phan Thi Kim Phuc was born and lived in a small village called Trang Bang located 25 miles west of the capital city Saigon in Vietnam.

On June 8, 1972, her village was being held by North Vietnamese forces. The Viet Cong had run a blockade across the highway that links Trang Bang to Saigon. The Viet Nam Air Force (VNAF) dropped napalm bombs (ignited jellied gasoline developed by our British allies in WWII, to knock out enemy troops in trenches and fortifications) outside the village, hitting the fortifications of the North Vietnamese Army (NVA).

The pilot saw people with weapons running towards the Army of the Republic of Viet Nam (ARVN) positions, where the journalists and photographers were also located. In a split-second decision to protect the ARVN troops from what he saw as a threat, the Vietnamese pilot diverted from his target and dove to attack the group. Kim's two cousins were killed and she was horribly burned. Her clothes burned from her body as she ran down the road in pain.

The Pulitzer Prize-winning image of terrified children (on the following page), including nine-year-old Kim Phuc, centre, as they run after an aerial napalm attack on their village, is etched in Associated Press (AP) photographer Nick Ut's memory. He carried Kim to the AP van and helped her family take her to the hospital. "This little girl came running out of the black smoke towards me, naked and screaming."

In Nick Ut's own words, "She was crying out, 'Non´g Qu´a! Non´g Qu´a! (Too hot! Too hot!).' Instinctively, I stepped back and clicked my camera. People were everywhere, fleeing from the fire and smoke that engulfed the area. I saw a woman carrying

a baby, screaming, 'Help! Help!' Another was running with a dead child in her arms. It was then that Kim and four other children came running towards me. With the help of some South Vietnamese soldiers, I poured water on the girl's badly burned body and carried her to the Associated Press van. She was crying in pain all the way to the Cu Chi hospital."

Kim was transferred to the elite Barsky burn clinic in Saigon, where, for months, she hovered between life and death. That was the beginning of the ordeal to save Kim Phuc. It would take 17 operations, the intervention of another photographer, Perry Kretz of *Stern* magazine, and numerous trips abroad for plastic surgery, before she could assume a "normal" life.

A New Life

The image of Kim running, which was often used to depict the horror of the Vietnam War, changed Kim's life and also formed a bond between her and Nick Ut. He revisited Vietnam during the 25th anniversary of the war's end and this time took pictures of a peaceful country.

In 1992, Kim Phuc came to Canada and in 1997 she took the Canadian citizenship test, earning a perfect score. When Canadians found out that the little girl from the 1972 photo was now a Canadian citizen, they raised $30 000 to help her settle in Canada. She has been declared a special ambassador to UNESCO. In 1997, she established the Kim Foundation, a not-for-profit organization to help children who are the victims of war.

Kim Phuc often speaks to groups of journalists. "Sometimes I like to think of that little girl, screaming, running up the road, as being not just a symbol of war, but a symbol of a cry for peace."

ACTIVITIES

DIRECTLY STATED IDEAS AND INFORMATION

1. Explain how this picture happened to be taken, and who took it.

2. What has Kim gone through since then, in order to lead a "normal" life?

INDIRECTLY STATED IDEAS AND INFORMATION

3. Explain why this photo received a Pulitzer Prize, in your opinion.

4. What did the photographer do immediately after taking this picture?

MAKING CONNECTIONS

5. What do you think about the role of photographers in areas of conflict and violence? Is it wrong to take pictures of people who are in need of immediate help? Or is the act of recording what is happening on film important enough that they do not need to offer assistance?

WRITING EXTENSION

Write a caption that could appear underneath this photo in a display of anti-war photography.

Address at the Vietnam War Memorial

❖ by Kim Phuc

November 11, 1996—Washington D.C.

Dear Friends:

I am very happy to be with you today. I thank you for giving me the opportunity to talk and meet with you on this Veterans' Day.

As you know I am the little girl who was running to escape from the napalm fire. I do not want to talk about the war because I cannot change history.

I only want you to remember the tragedy of war in order to do things to stop fighting and killing around the world.

I have suffered a lot from both physical and emotional pain. Sometimes I thought I could not live, but God saved me and gave me faith and hope.

Even if I could talk face to face with the pilot who dropped the bombs, I would tell him we cannot change history but we should try to do good things for the present and for the future to promote peace.

I did not think that I could marry nor have any children because of my burns, but now I have a wonderful husband and lovely son and a happy family.

Dear friends, I just dream one day people all over the world can live in real peace—no fighting, and no hostility. We should work together to build peace and happiness for all people in all nations.

Thank you so much for letting me be a part of this important day.

ACTIVITIES

DIRECTLY STATED IDEAS AND INFORMATION

1. Why does the speaker not want to talk about war? What does she want to talk about?

2. How has her life turned out?

INDIRECTLY STATED IDEAS AND INFORMATION

3. Why do you think Kim Phuc has such a positive attitude?

4. What is Kim Phuc's message to her audience? What is the most important idea she wants to get across?

MAKING CONNECTIONS

5. What makes this speaker's words so powerful?

WRITING EXTENSION

Write a news report as if you have just heard this speech at the United States Vietnam War Memorial, and you are reporting on her message. Use appropriate quotations from her text.

READING STRATEGY

This poem was written by a Grade 12 student. As you read through the poem, notice the arrangement of words on each line.

VOCABULARY PREVIEW

- innocent
- recover
- therapy
- powerful
- door gunner
- overcoming

Forgiveness

❖ by Jennifer Boehm

It all happened so fast.
I was an innocent nine-year-old girl,
I had no clue . . .
All I remember is
that plane up in the sky,
it kept dropping bombs
down on my home land.

Up in flames, my body stinging
I strip myself away from my burning
clothing.
I am running in terror and fear,
all I want is to be home again.
But I'm all alone, I just want my family
to comfort me.

Doctors and nurses helping me recover
two years of therapy . . .
I am grateful to be here today,
sharing my personal story.
Hoping that war will never return

I believe in God.
My picture has given me a powerful gift,
crying and working for peace.
I will forgive the little boy,
who was the door gunner.

Although the world is full of suffering,
it is also full of the overcoming of it
with forgiveness.

ACTIVITIES

DIRECTLY STATED IDEAS AND INFORMATION

1. From whose point of view is this poem written?

2. What specific details of Kim Phuc's experience are mentioned in this poem?

INDIRECTLY STATED IDEAS AND INFORMATION

3. What emotions has the student writer emphasized in this poem?

4. What does the narrator mean when she says, "My picture has given me a powerful gift"?

MAKING CONNECTIONS

5. "Although the world is full of suffering, it is also full of the overcoming of it." What examples of the goodness of people can you think of that restore your own positive outlook?

WRITING EXTENSION

Write your own poem in response to the photograph of Kim Phuc. If you have not already done so, you may want to read "Kim Phuc" on pages 223–224 to find out more about the story behind the photograph.

The Bully

❖ by Gregory Clark

Aubrey was his name. He could have been about eight or nine years of age. I was about seven.

He would lie in wait for me on my way to school. Four times every day. Being at that time a very small, measly little boy consisting largely of freckles, knuckles, knees and feet, I believed devoutly in the principle of non-resistance. Even before I started to school, I had learned I could not run fast enough to escape predators among my fellow-beings. Nor had I the weight, speed or courage to fight when overtaken.

Aubrey was a large, loose boy with sallow skin, pale eyes, a nasal voice and a frustrated character. Nobody loved him. The teachers didn't like him. He was avoided in the schoolyard. In the knots and squads of children going to and coming from school, Aubrey, large and louty for his age, was always mauling, pushing, shoving the smaller kids. The groups would either hurry to leave him behind or stop and wait for him to go on. Nobody, nobody loved him.

Then he found me. I fancy he lived two blocks closer to the school than I. He would wait for me just around a corner. He would lie in wait in side alleys, lanes, behind hedges. As Aubrey was large for his age, I was small for mine. I found difficulty joining the right gangs of children heading to or from school. I, like Aubrey, found myself often walking alone.

Aubrey would throw me down and kneel on me, his knees on my biceps. He would glare down at me out of his pale eyes with a look of triumph. He would pretend he was going to spit on me. He would grind his fist on my nose, not too heavy, but revelling in the imagined joy of punching somebody on the nose. It was inexpressible pleasure to him to have somebody at his mercy.

I tried starting to school late; lingering at school after dismissal. I tried going new ways, around strange blocks. No use, Aubrey got me. I had no protectors. My father was a fighting man, who would have laughed if I had revealed to him my terror. "Why," he would have cried gaily, "punch him in the nose!"

After about two years, Aubrey vanished. I suppose his family moved away. But as the years came and went, like ever-rising waves of the tide of life and experience, my memory kept Aubrey alive. As I grew, the memory of Aubrey was my age too. When I was twenty, there in my life still lived the large, sallow, cruel figure of Aubrey. My hatred of him matured, became adult, took on the known shape of a presence.

In the Vimy battle, by 8:30 a.m., I was the only officer left in my company. I had started, three hours earlier, the baby lieutenant. Now I was alone with 200 men.

Orders came, now that we had reached the crest and the last final wonderful objective, that the R.C.R., having been held up at a semi-final objective, there was a gap on our left between us and the Princess Pats.

"You will take the necessary party," orders said, "and bomb across to meet a party from the Patricias, which will start from their flank at 9 a.m.. You should attempt to meet their party half-way across."

"Who," I said to my sergeant, Charlie Windsor, "will I take with me?"

It was a pretty dreadful time. It was sleeting. The air shook with shell fire, whistled and spat with machine-gun fire and without shape of form, random monsters fell around us, belching up gray earth, gray smoke, gray men.

"Me" answered Sgt. Windsor, "and five others."

We got the canvas buckets and filled them with bombs. Sgt. Windsor got a Lewis gun and five pans for it. At 9 a.m., peering across the grisly expanse toward where the Patricias should be, we saw sure enough, a glimpse of furtive forms, half a dozen of them, bobbing, dodging, vanishing, reappearing. They were coming toward us.

"They've already started!" said Sgt. Windsor, hoisting the Lewis.

"Let's go," I croaked.

So, bobbing, dodging, vanishing, reappearing ourselves, we seven headed out to meet the Pats half-way. Down into shell craters, up over crater lips; down into the next craters, pools, mud, fresh hot holes, charred and new-burned, big holes, little holes, we slithered and slid and crouched. Two or three times Sgt. Windsor had to slide the nozzle of the Lewis over the lip of craters and spray half a pan of fire into brush clumps. And once into a tree, half-way up, out of which a gray sack fell, heavily.

But each time up, we saw the Pats coming to us. And their bombs rang nearer, and ours rang nearer to them. We now could hear each other's shouts of encouragement and greeting.

"One more spurt!" I assured my crew.

The Pats squad was led by a long-geared, rangy man for whom I felt sorry each time I glimpsed him coming toward us. A pity all men can't be half-pints at war!

Our next plunge would be the last. We could hear the Pats only a few yards away.

Out over the lip I crouched and hurtled, feet first. Feet first I slid into a big crater, and over its lip skidded feet first the rangy, long-geared Pat.

You're right. It was Aubrey.

His pale eyes stared incredulous and triumphant down into mine. His sallow face split in a muddy grin.

"Don't I know you, sir?" he puffed.

"You sure should," I sighed struggling erect as possible and holding out my hand.

Hate dies funny.

ACTIVITIES

DIRECTLY STATED IDEAS AND INFORMATION

1. How does the narrator say that his father would have reacted to Aubrey's bullying?

2. Why does the narrator feel sorry for the leader of the Pats?

INDIRECTLY STATED IDEAS AND INFORMATION

3. How have the tables turned when these two men meet again during the war?

4. What does the narrator mean when he says, "Hate dies funny"?

MAKING CONNECTIONS

5. Why do you think that Aubrey bullied the narrator?

WRITING EXTENSION

Summarize the narrator's experience with Aubrey in one paragraph.

READING STRATEGY

Before you read this selection, jot down a list of words that you think describe Canada's peacekeepers overseas. As you read, check your list to see whether the examples given reflect the same ideas you noted.

I am Canadian . . .

❖ by Master Corporal Frank Misztal

VOCABULARY PREVIEW

◆ combats
◆ fatigues
◆ trench
◆ foxhole
◆ bilingual
◆ deployed
◆ humanity
◆ occupy
◆ harmony
◆ ambassador

- I wear combats, not fatigues and I work for a "lef-tenant," not a "loo-tenant."

- I drive an Iltis, not a Jeep or a Humvee, and the weapon I carry for my protection is a C7, not an M16.

- I observe from, or take cover in, a trench and not a foxhole.

- I don't just speak English or French, nor am I bilingual. I can speak many languages.

- Although I am trained to fight in a war, I don't cause them.

- When I am not deployed on a mission of peace, I travel all over my country; fighting forest fires, battling floods, rescuing lost souls or repairing damages caused by an ice storm.

- I try not to take sides and believe in treating all humanity equally.

- I don't just go on patrols; I also clear landmines to make the area safe for everyone.

- In my off-duty hours while deployed, I occupy myself by rebuilding schools or playgrounds, and I teach children in a war-torn country about peace and harmony.

- I am my country's best ambassador and I am respected the world over for what I do best.

- I carry my country's flag shamelessly and hold my head up high wherever I go.

- My name is Frank, and I am . . . a proud Canadian peacekeeper.

ACTIVITIES

DIRECTLY STATED IDEAS AND INFORMATION

1. What roles do Canadian peacekeepers play besides combat roles? Make a list based on information in the text.

2. Make a chart like the one below to list differences in terminology that distinguish Canadian peacekeepers.

Canadian Term	Other Term

INDIRECTLY STATED IDEAS AND INFORMATION

3. What do you think the author is trying to accomplish by writing this text?

4. What is the author's attitude toward children of other countries? How can you tell?

MAKING CONNECTIONS

5. What different types of training would be required to do this job well? Write a bulleted list.

WRITING EXTENSION

What do you feel sets you and other Canadians apart? Write your own version of "I am Canadian . . ." Include at least seven points.

READING STRATEGY

Before you read this selection, think about why someone your age might want to join the army. Jot down all the reasons in favour of such a move that you can think of. As you read, see if your ideas match those of the author.

G.I. Jane?

❖ by Veronica T.

VOCABULARY PREVIEW

- ◆ discipline
- ◆ exposure
- ◆ peacekeeper
- ◆ recruitment
- ◆ gigantic
- ◆ podium
- ◆ intimidated
- ◆ physical
- ◆ Regular Officer Training Plan
- ◆ Boot Camp

One day I was sitting on the bus in Toronto and I saw an ad for the Canadian Armed Forces. I stared at it for probably 10 minutes. I could picture myself there, in the army, and I found myself making a decision. "I'm joining the army," I said to my mom when I got home.

Okay, so it was a bit of a surprise. But I really don't see anything bad about me joining the army. They would pay for me to attend any university across Canada, the training will keep me in great shape, I'll be healthy, I'll learn skills there that I wouldn't learn anywhere else, and the experience I'll get will be amazing! The discipline that I would get there, the people I would meet and places I would see when I am done school would give me great exposure to the rest of the world. I could be sent to different places in Europe, or I may be stationed somewhere in Canada, just as a peacekeeper.

Since Canada is a peacekeeping country, our armed forces don't actually fight but they do patrol at riots and provide order and aid. As many of the countries Canadian soldiers travel to are at war, it is still a dangerous job.

Of course when I tell people about my plan, they think I am crazy. But I ignored everything people said to me and I went to speak to my guidance counsellor about it. He gave me the number and address of the Armed Forces recruitment centre in Toronto, and I went there that very afternoon. (My mother made me swear not to sign any papers before she got to read all of them.) The brown building north of Toronto was gigantic and I was a bit nervous about going in, but I did. I looked around and saw a man standing behind a podium. He looked mean and I was truly intimidated, but then I looked around and saw a table of young guys that I assumed were joining the army. I could

see that they thought I was crazy for being there. Of course, I had to sit at the table where the guys were sitting. I felt awkward and I wouldn't even cross my legs. I sat like them. I was completely fascinated with everything in it when I heard one of the guys whisper to his friend, "Oh yeah, I can just see her, 'Ohmigod, I broke a nail!'" I wanted to say some smart remark to him but I didn't bother. I could not believe that was what they thought. I was there for the same reason that they were, but because I am a female they figure that I can't handle it.

An officer came over and started talking to all of us. He was explaining how first we have to have an interview, then a physical, and a test before you get in. I was given booklets and a sheet with some of the interview questions, like "Why do you want to join the army, why should we take you,

what do you hope to get from the army," etc. The questions are similar to those of any job interview. The program that I want to go into is called Regular Officer Training Plan (ROTP). It starts off with 10 weeks of "Boot Camp," then after that, if I survive, I will go to Humber College—which they pay for—and after I graduate from college I serve them for three years as an officer.

Now does that sound like a bad deal? By the age of 24 I will have finished all of my schooling and already served three years for the armed forces. I can stay with them longer if I want to, but even short term will give me a chance to explore and experience different things. Joining the army will benefit me in a lot of ways. I still have one more year left of high school before I sign up, but I can say that it will be an experience I will never forget.

ACTIVITIES

DIRECTLY STATED IDEAS AND INFORMATION

1. What does the author see as the possible benefits of joining the army?

2. Describe the process for joining the army in your own words.

INDIRECTLY STATED IDEAS AND INFORMATION

3. What assumptions does "G.I. Jane" make about being in the armed forces?

4. What was the attitude of the male candidates toward this female candidate?

MAKING CONNECTIONS

5. Does the author appear to have thought this decision through carefully? Why?

WRITING EXTENSION

Make a chart of pros and cons of joining the Canadian Armed Forces, as if you were this young woman.

READING STRATEGY

Use the **SQ3R** (Survey, Question, Read, Recite, Review) technique to help retain the information in this selection.
1. **Survey:** Scan the headings in the selection.
2. **Question:** Read over the questions at the end of the selection to see if you can answer them.
3. **Read** the selection and take notes. Try to include the most important information given under each heading. Use a chart like the one below to record your information.

Text Headings	Notes

4. **Recite:** Working in pairs, go through the notes you just made. For each heading or subheading, one of you should read your summary notes. The other one should listen and add additional information as necessary. Take turns being the summarizer.
5. **Review:** Go through your notes and outline the main points in the text.

VOCABULARY PREVIEW

- accommodation
- concentrations
- enhance
- certification
- potential

Travel Counsellors

What They Do
- Provide travel information to individuals/groups regarding destinations, transportation, and accommodation options/travel costs, and recommend suitable products
- Plan and organize vacation travel for individuals or groups
- Make transportation/accommodation reservations using a computerized reservation/ticketing system
- Sell single-fare tickets and packaged tours
- Promote particular destinations, tour packages, and other travel services
- Investigate new travel destinations, hotels, and other facilities/attractions
- Provide travel tips regarding tourist attractions, foreign currency, customs, languages, and travel safety
- Travel counsellors work in travel agencies, hotel chains, and transportation/tourism firms.
- The highest concentrations (per 10 000 people) of travel counsellors are found in Ontario and British Columbia while the lowest concentrations are in Prince Edward Island and Newfoundland.

What You Need

- You usually need a high school diploma. A college diploma or vocational training in travel or tourism is also usually required.
- You may need certification with the ACTA/CITC's (Alliance of Canadian Travel Association and Canadian Institute of Travel Counsellors) Canadian Educational Standards System (ACCESS). This certification requires three years' experience in the industry and the completion of mandatory courses/examinations.
- With experience, you may move up the ranks to become a manager.
- Most recent entrants have a community college diploma, and almost one in five has an undergraduate university degree.

Required/Related Educational Programs

- Sports and Recreation
- Commerce—Business Administration
- Psychology

*These educational programs are listed in the order in which they are most likely to supply graduates to this occupation.

Useful Experience/Skills

- Dealing with the public
- Customer service
- Computer use
- Scheduling

Useful High School Subjects

- English
- Geography
- Computer Basics
- Business

Current Conditions

Your work prospects are rated FAIR because:

- The employment growth rate is generally below average, and earnings potential is low.
- Hourly wages ($13.41) are below average ($16.91), although the rate of wage growth is above average.
- The unemployment rate (4.4%) is about average (5%).
- A greater-than-average number of job seekers are immigrants, and few new entrants are recent graduates.

Outlook to 2007

Your work prospects will continue to be rated FAIR because:

- The employment growth rate will generally be above average, but earnings potential should remain low.
- The retirement rate will likely be about average, and the number of retiring workers should contribute to job openings.
- The number of job seekers will likely match the number of job openings, although the supply of new graduates is below average.

Preparing for the Competition

- You're likely to be more successful if you have "people" skills and can deliver good customer service.

Work Prospects

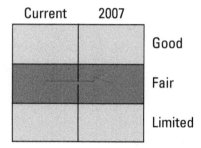

What You Can Expect to Make

- Earnings are close to the average for occupations in the sales and service sectors and for all intermediate occupations.
- These wages grew at an above-average rate from 1999 to 2001.

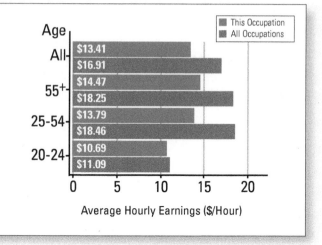

Average Hourly Earnings ($/Hour)

Legend: ■ This Occupation ■ All Occupations

Age	This Occupation	All Occupations
All	$13.41	$16.91
55+	$14.47	$18.25
25-54	$13.79	$18.46
20-24	$10.69	$11.09

ACTIVITIES

DIRECTLY STATED IDEAS AND INFORMATION

1. According to the bar graph titled "What You Can Expect to Make," how do the hourly wages for travel counsellors compare with those for other occupations?

2. Which educational program supplies the most graduates to the Travel Counsellor industry?

INDIRECTLY STATED IDEAS AND INFORMATION

3. Explain why work prospects for travel counsellors are described as "fair."

4. Where are the highest concentrations of travel counsellors found geographically? Explain why this might be the case.

MAKING CONNECTIONS

5. Would you be interested in being a travel counsellor? Support your answer with information from the selection.

WRITING EXTENSION

Write a letter of application to a travel agency to apply for a job as a travel counsellor. Make sure you outline the skills you have that would make you good at the job.

READING STRATEGY

*This career profile comes from a geography textbook. Make a **KWL chart** (see page 32) and write what you know about being an "ecotourism entrepreneur." After you have read the selection, fill in as many answers as you can in the third column.*

Ecotourism Entrepreneur

❖ by Colin M. Bain

VOCABULARY PREVIEW

◆ entrepreneur
◆ motivate
◆ ecotourism
◆ virtually
◆ originality
◆ creative thinking
◆ vital
◆ venture
◆ exporting

Name: Bruce Poon Tip
High School: Henry Wisewood High School, Calgary, Alberta
Job Title: Ecotourism Entrepreneur

What I like about my work:
"I love the benefits I can bring to local communities by sending tourists there who will respect their culture. I love employing people who support the idea of sustainable tourism. I love having a global impact because of the decisions I make."

Being a successful entrepreneur requires a special kind of person. An entrepreneur is someone who runs his or her own business. You need to be able to motivate yourself, you need to be willing to work long hours, and you need to be willing to risk everything you have. But the rewards can be great, as Bruce Poon Tip has discovered.

Bruce started to work in the fast-food industry when he left high school. But he soon realized that he did not really want to work for someone else. So after completing a diploma at Mount Royal

College in Calgary, he opened his own ecotourism company (GAP Adventures) at the age of twenty-one.

By working with similar companies in other parts of the world, Bruce's company can offer tours virtually anywhere. In turn, other ecotourism companies can send clients to Canada, where Bruce will organize tours to see polar bears in Churchill, Manitoba, or canoe trips in the Northwest Territories.

Bruce believes that originality and creative thinking are vital for the success of any business venture. These qualities have certainly worked for him. In January 2002, Bruce was the only Canadian operator invited to attend the United Nations launch of the Year of Ecotourism in New York. He has won many awards, including the government's Global Traders Leadership award for his groundbreaking ideas in exporting services.

> How a knowledge of geography helps me in my job:
> *"Thinking globally has got me where I am now. Geography has taught me what makes parts of the world unique."*

ACTIVITIES

DIRECTLY STATED IDEAS AND INFORMATION

1. What training did Bruce need to become an ecotourism guide?

2. What qualities does Bruce feel are necessary to become a successful entrepreneur?

INDIRECTLY STATED IDEAS AND INFORMATION

3. How does Bruce's work show his creative thinking?

4. What are the benefits of being an entrepreneur? What are the drawbacks?

MAKING CONNECTIONS

5. What qualities other than those mentioned in the text do you think you would need to work in this job?

WRITING EXTENSION

Do you have what it takes to be an entrepreneur? Why or why not? Write a self-assessment paragraph in answer to this question.

READING STRATEGY
Look at this selection from a distance. What do you think is being advertised?

SUV Ad

ACTIVITIES

DIRECTLY STATED IDEAS AND INFORMATION

1. What type of vehicle is featured in the ad? Why?

INDIRECTLY STATED IDEAS AND INFORMATION

2. Explain why the vehicle is shown driving through a desert.

3. If the author believes that SUVs cause environmental damage, why does the ad say that nature will "grow back"?

4. Explain the purpose of using different typefaces throughout this selection. What type of ad is it trying to copy? Why?

MAKING CONNECTIONS

5. Do you think this is an effective ad? Provide reasons for your point of view.

WRITING EXTENSION

Write a letter to the editor of a newspaper in which this ad has appeared. Explain your response to the ad.

If everyone worked hard to help
the people in their own lives, imagine
what a better world this would be.

— *Craig Kielburger (b. 1982)*
Youth Activist

READING STRATEGY

Before you read this ad, brainstorm a list of ads you have seen that focus more on the image of the company itself than on the products being sold. Is this a common form of advertising?

Ford Ad

When fires in Mexico destroyed 490,000 acres of forest and 870,000 acres of grassland, Ford Motor Company, our dealers, and the government of Mexico joined together to plant more than 3 million trees in an effort to bring the ecosystem back into balance.

Land Lover Karen Arguello is part of our public affairs team. She put Ford and the Mexican government in the woods together.

Ford Motor Company

ACTIVITIES

DIRECTLY STATED IDEAS AND INFORMATION

1. Why were 3 million trees planted in Mexico?

2. Who was the Ford employee who spearheaded the tree-planting effort?

INDIRECTLY STATED IDEAS AND INFORMATION

3. Explain the purpose of the statement "Sometimes they can't see the forest, period."

4. What is the purpose of the visual feature in the top right corner of this selection?

MAKING CONNECTIONS

5. Explain why the Ford Motor Company is advertising their commitment to the environment.

WRITING EXTENSION

Based upon the information contained in this selection and details you make up, write a newspaper article that describes the tree planting done by Ford in Mexico. Make sure you include the most important information and add a quote for realism.

Reflecting on Your Learning

This section will give you a chance to think back over the past unit, reflect upon what you have learned, and apply it to your future learning.

READING SKILLS

1. Which reading strategy that you used in this unit was most helpful? Why? Find another selection in the unit that you think this strategy would have helped you to understand.

2. Find two pieces in this unit that have a different tone, and write two words to describe it (e.g., humorous, angry, serious). How is the tone appropriate to the subject and audience?

WRITING /COMMUNICATION SKILLS

3. Use a Venn diagram to compare 2 writing tasks you completed for this unit.

   Writing task 1: _____   Writing task 2: _____

   differences   similarities   differences

4. With a partner, compare notes on the process you used to write one of the assignments in this unit. Is there anything that your partner did that you think you might try yourself?

LEARNING SKILLS

5. Give three examples of how reading skills can improve your writing, or how writing skills can improve your reading.

LOOKING AHEAD

6. What communication skills have you learned in this course that will help you in your life? Explain how you plan to use these skills in the future.

Text and Figure Credits

Guenther Zuern, *Ontario Reader*, Newcomer Communications, 2003. Copyright © 2003 Newcomer Communications; **216-217** "The Real McCoy" by Bev Spencer from *Made in Canada: 101 Amazing Achievements* by Bev Spencer, Scholastic Canada, 2003. Copyright © 2003 by Bev Spencer. All rights reserved; **218-219** "Safer Hockey" by Bev Spencer from *Made in Canada: 101 Amazing Achievements* by Bev Spencer, Scholastic Canada, 2003. Copyright © 2003 by Bev Spencer. All rights reserved; **220-221** "Teens Make Their Own Peace" by Leah Eskin. From *Scholastic Update*, March 1989. Copyright Scholastic Inc.; **223-224** "Kim Phuc" by David M.R.D. Spencer from Spencer, David M.R.D. "The Kim Phuc Story", CanadianIdentity.com. Erin, Ontario. 2003 <http://www.canadianidentity.com/p/kim_phuc>;

226-227 "Address at the Vietnam War Memorial" by Kim Phuc. Copyright © 1996 Kim Phuc; **228-229** "Forgiveness" by Jennifer Boehm. Copyright © 2003 Jennifer Boehm; **230-233** "The Bully" by Gregory Clark. Copyright © 1964 Gregory Clark; **234-235** "I am Canadian" by Master Corporal Frank Misztal. Copyright © 2004 Frank Misztal. Kingston, ON, Canada; **236-237** "G.I. Jane?" by Veronica T., Brampton, ON. From *TG Magazine*. Reprinted by permission of the publisher; **239-241** "Travel Counsellors" from *Travel Counsellors* (NOC 6431), Human Resources Development Canada. Reproduced with the permission of the Minister of Public Works and Government Services Canada, 2003; **242-243** "Ecotourism Entrepreneur" by Colin M. Bain. From *Experience Canada*. Copyright © Oxford University Press (Canada) 2003.

Photo Credits

AP=Associated Press
CP=CP Picture Archive

2-3 Digital Vision; **16** V.C.L./Getty Images; **33** AP/Wide World Photos; **41** © AFP/CORBIS/MAGMA; **62** © Reuters NewMedia Inc./CORBIS/MAGMA; **67** National Eating Disorders Information Centre, 200 Elizabeth St., Toronto; **69** Courtesy of Kellogg Canada, © 1997; **72** From *Haunted Canada: True Ghost Stories* by Pat Hancock, Scholastic Canada, 2003. All Photos by Jennifer MacKinnon; **80-81** Keren Su/Getty Images; **86** © Daryl Benson/Masterfile; **88** CP/Toronto Star (Boris Spremo); **91-93** Copyright © United Way of Kitchener-Waterloo and Area; **102** © Paul Seheult; Eye Ubiquitous/CORBIS/MAGMA; **115** Andrew Stawicki/Toronto Star; **117** Al Harvey/The Slide Farm; **123** Leonard Frank, photographer. Japanese Canadian National Museum / Alec Eastwood Collection

94/69.4.16.; **142** Copyright © 2003 The Hamilton Spectator; **150-152** All photos courtesy of Thrasher Magazine; **168-169** Daly & Newton/The Image Bank/Getty Images; **174** © CORBIS/MAGMA; **184** The Far Side® by Gary Larson © 1982 FarWorks, Inc. All Rights Reserved. Used with permission; **191** Charles T. Webber, *The Underground Railroad*, Cincinnati Art Museum, Subscription Fund Purchase, Acc. 1927.26; **192** Ontario Black History Society; **194** AP/Wide World Photos; **195** AP/Wide World Photos; **196** Courtesy Reebok Human Rights Foundation; **202** Copyright © 2004 Daily Bread Food Bank, creative by Lowe RMP; **205** © CORBIS/MAGMA; **210** © CORBIS/MAGMA; **213** CP(Jeff McIntosh); **224** AP/Wide World Photos; **228** AP/Wide World Photos; **237** © Anna Clopet/CORBIS/MAGMA; **242** Courtesy of Bruce Poon Tip; **244** Copyright 1996 Abrupt. Republished here courtesy of Abrupt, www.abrupt.org; **246-247** Ford Motor Company.